Volleyball – A Handbook for Coaches and Players

ρ̄οδος
2400 χρόνια

Dedicated to the city
of Rhodos, on the occasion
of its 2400-year jubilee,
and also to the island
on which this manual
was realised.

Athanasios Papageorgiou/Willy Spitzley
Assistance: Rainer Christ

Volleyball

– A Handbook
for Coaches and Players

Meyer & Meyer Sport

Contents

1 The Book and the Game

Introduction

Success in the game of volleyball depends on 2 factors, firstly the ability to play the game, i.e. the mastery of the various skills, tactics and strategies involved in the game and secondly, and as important, enjoyment. These 2 factors a closely inter-linked as a player who has little or no skill will probably get little enjoyment from playing and may, as a consequence, give the game up early on. One of the aims of coaching is not only to introduce players to a sport, but also to sustain their interest such that they may fulfil their potential, and therefore one of the aims of the coach is to teach the elements of the game in a way that is both enjoyable and satisfying to the student, and in such a way that all the stated learning objectives are achieved.

The Purpose of this Book

This book is intended for coaches who have a good grasp of the game in terms of the basic rules, and terminology involved in teaching and coaching.

The prime objective of this book is to help the coach take his students from foundation to performance level. In other words, over time, to produce a mature, thinking player, who can not only select and apply the appropriate response at the correct time, but understands the rules of the game and applies these within the spirit of the game. The author has many years experience of both teaching and coaching the game, experience that has given rise to both the coaching method used, and the order of the learning outcomes. Indeed if it is looked at in a linear format the proposed development pattern follows that outlined in Fig. 1 below.

Foundation level   Introduction to mini-volleyball

Participation level   developing an allround recreative player, capable of playing the game to club level

Performance level   developing a high quality competitive player, capable of playing the game at county level and above

Fig. 1

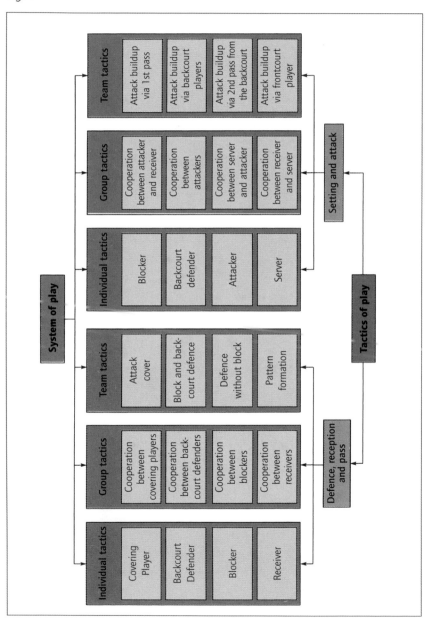

The major difference between playing the game at mini and club level and performing at high level is the degree of complexity, the speed and accuracy demanded of the players. In other words, the basic skills and tactics of the game are very similar, but it is the speed, power, and consistency and overall quality of play that are the hallmarks of the performance player.

The way this book is designed is that the skills and tactics taught at mini-volleyball level, namely movement in relation to the ball, targets, other players (both opponents and team-mates) are translated easily and effortlessly into the full game. The key message of this book is that the skills and tactics must be acquired in the context of the game and not in isolation and always in keeping with the rules and spirit of the game. Thus ensuring players that have a cognitive appreciation of what they are being called on to do, can respond not only quickly, but also flexibly. In fact at the early stage of a player's development it is very important for the coach to work on the general rather than specific positional play.

Learning Objectives

The book includes 16 learning objectives, which takes the student from mini-volleyball to performance player. Each individual objective is clearly defined, and includes:

- A scene setting section.
- 2 or 3 session plans each of which contains developmental skill and tactical practices.
- Examples of problems that may occur plus suggested solutions.

The Game

Volleyball is a game that is suitable for both sexes and for players of all ages and abilities and can be adapted to allow players with a physical or mental disability to play at competitive level. Players of all ages, or a serious competitive sport can play it as part of a learning experience, for example as part of the school curriculum or as a recreative activity.

In terms of the taxonomy of sports, volleyball is essentially a court game, very similar in structure to the game of tennis. It is played by teams of 6 players on a relatively small court of dimensions 9 x 18 metres, which is sub-divided into 2 playing areas of 9 x 9 metres, divided by a net of 2.43 metres in height (2.24

metres for women). In other words the opponents, as in tennis, play on either side of a net with no physical contact, but allowing one team to dominate another by restricting their freedom of action by power and speed of play. However, where it differs from tennis is the tactical and strategic complexity of the game that results from the fact that it is played by a team of players, each with his own positional responsibility. Therefore volleyball is normally classified as a team game.

At this stage, without going in depth into the specifics of the game, a simple explanation is that the aim of volleyball is to place the ball in the opponent's court in such a position and manner that they cannot return it, or even successfully keep the ball in play. One important rule in volleyball is the fact that a team has only 3 touches to get the ball into a scoring position. This means that transposition from attack to defence takes place very quickly, for example, each phase of the game lasts approximately 8-12 seconds. The team that is not in possession of the ball has the aim of not only defending successfully but must be ready to initiate an attack when they gain possession of the ball.

Volleyball is a game that is not played within a finite time frame such as soccer, but because of its structure a match may last for several hours. The game is played to 5 sets and the introduction of a tiebreaker means that the game cannot be drawn. This innovation was introduced, like so much in modern sport, to increase the game's media appeal.

The Rules

The rules of the game impact on the techniques, skills, tactics and strategies that the coach may employ. According to the change in rules in 1994:

1. The service zone was extended from 3 metres to 9 metres.
2. A player is allowed to contact the ball with any part of the body.
3. Double contact is permitted during defence and ball saving actions.

These changes have served to strengthen the defensive phases of play. (Additional rule changes have been introduced since the completion of his book and these are included on page 42). The rules of volleyball mean that compared with other team sports the transition from attack to defence and vice versa is not only quicker but also more frequent. It also means that rarely does a player have an offensive and defensive function simultaneously. For example, when a player is spiking, his team-mates cover the potential counter-attack.

Offence/Defence
One of the most important rules concerns the area of the court from which an attacking move may be made. The court is divided into 4 tactical areas, a front/attacking court and a back/defensive court, each of which is divided into 2 areas related to the service. In line with these divisions there are two types of player front/attackers and back/defenders. The relevance of this demarcation is that no defending player may make a direct attack into the opponent's court or "goal", either as an attacker or a "blocker". Therefore, the initial position and rotation of players on the court is important.

Rotation
This rule states that the team winning the right to serve must rotate the players one position clockwise. Obviously this means that all players must be able to play both attacking and defending roles with the concomitant techniques, skills and tactics involved in this change. The referee has overall discretion regarding the validity of contact, and may call a foul if he considers that the ball was "carried" which makes the skill and anticipation even more difficult for the players.

Ball Contact
In volleyball a team is limited to 3 ball contacts in succession, which means that no player (except the blocker) may touch the ball more than once. Therefore each player must make all decisions regarding the next play before contacting the ball. This calls for very high levels of anticipation and the ability to "read" the game. Finally, ball contact must be percussive; i.e. it must rebound immediately off the hand and not be "carried" on the player's hand. This increases the skill level of the game in that to achieve success, i.e. to hit the opponent's goal area or court requires both accuracy and speed of implementation.

Tacticts – an Overview

The pace of volleyball is very fast (see above) and consists of repeated jumps, dives and changes of direction over a relatively short distance, for example, 3-6m maximum.

As with all games, the objective is for each team to try to gain tactical supremacy in a fast changing situation and the fact that there are only 3 touches allowed makes this all the more difficult. It is true to say that because of the strictures of time and touch, volleyball is one of the most skilful team games. As with all games, tactics are divided into three phases:

1. Offence
2. Defence
3. Transposition or transition between the two

In terms of a tactical analysis of the game there are 2 basic situations:

1. The 1st ball contact, i.e. defence/reception/pass
2. Setting and attack (2nd and 3rd ball contact)

As previously described above, the game allows for only 3 touches before attempting to score a point in the opponent's court in such a way that this may be in the form of a straight point, or in putting so much pressure on the opposition that they cannot keep the ball in play. However, should they be able to do so then the first phase of transition from defence to attack is the first contact. Some people might feel that this means that the game is primarily one of offence, with little defensive play involved. It is vital to defend a potential counter-attack in order to initiate the next attacking move. This situation is made easier if the opponent's ball was high and slow, because this gives more time to read, position and decide on a response. If, on the other hand, the ball is hit hard and fast, a player has less time to process information and make a decision as to his response. In this case the player's prime objectives are to defend, to keep the ball in play and if possible to set up the next attacking play, leading naturally to the first phase attack.

Following the first defensive contact/touch described above, come the second and third contacts with the ball. During this phase, the team is preparing to score by hitting the ball into their opponent's court. To do this the players must set the ball up for the spike/smash to score on the third contact/touch.
This may be done in several ways:

1. If the player has the time and skill the first touch may, in fact, be a set.
2. Failing this, or under the pressure from the opponents, the second touch may be an attacking touch, but not a set.
3. Normally it is essential that the second touch is the set, ready to spike/smash the ball into the opponent's court.

Tactics – Applied

In order to understand and learn how to cope with these pressure situations, it is important for players to be coached in the structures and patterns of volleyball.

These are described as three elements or units of play:

- Individual tactics, i.e. the learned responses of an individual player which take place under the pressure of external and internal stimuli. It is vital for successful individual tactics that the player has a good repertoire of skills on which to draw. It is the skill of each individual player that contributes to
- Group tactics, i.e. moves that involve a number of players (between 2 and 5) who aim to execute the team tactic and get the team out of trouble.
- Team tactics, i.e. moves that involve all 6 players who work cohesively to achieve a corporate goal or setting up a successful attack. Team tactics create the framework in which individual and group actions take place.

It is these units that form a system of play that contributes to team tactics as a whole. Fig. 2 on the next pages illustrates the interrelationship between these three units of play and the overall team tactics in a simple diagrammatic system of play.

A System of Play

Fig. 2

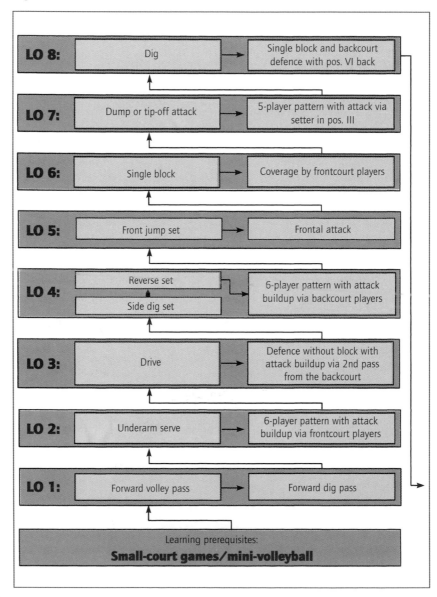

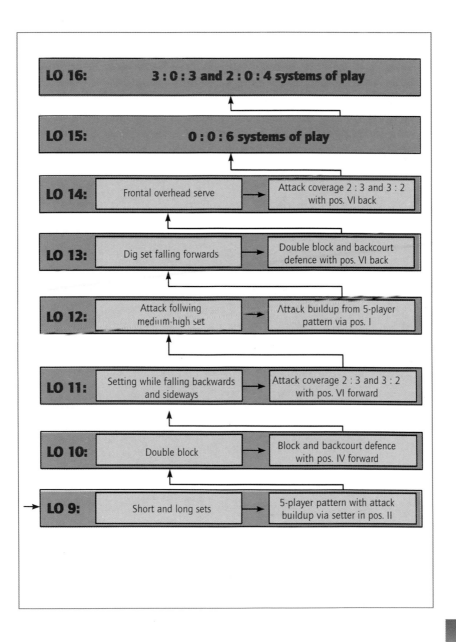

LO 16: 3 : 0 : 3 and 2 : 0 : 4 systems of play

LO 15: 0 : 0 : 6 systems of play

LO 14: Frontal overhead serve → Attack coverage 2 : 3 and 3 : 2 with pos. VI back

LO 13: Dig set falling forwards → Double block and backcourt defence with pos. VI back

LO 12: Attack follwing medium-high set → Attack buildup from 5-player pattern via pos. I

LO 11: Setting while falling backwards and sideways → Attack coverage 2 : 3 and 3 : 2 with pos. VI forward

LO 10: Double block → Block and backcourt defence with pos. IV forward

LO 9: Short and long sets → 5-player pattern with attack buildup via setter in pos. II

The Player

Volleyball players can be any shape or size, but those who are going to reach performance level are tall, fast in terms of speed of both reaction and movement, agile, well-balanced and co-ordinated, flexible and with the ability to spring/jump.

In other words, the high-level player requires the speed to respond to balls that are travelling up to 80-130 km/h and move very quickly; the power to spring repeatedly at the net and to hit the ball in such as way as to make a return impossible, or to block an opponent's smash; the flexibility to move from standing to diving and rolling to retrieve a ball; the co-ordination to move smoothly between one action and the next and finally the endurance, to keep going for the duration of the match. Because of the structure and rules of the game it is essential that players must not only be in good physical condition, but also have a long attention span and be mentally tough enough to sustain their physical output over a protracted period of time. Additionally, the player needs to be able to accurately observe the run of play in order that they can anticipate or read the game such that they can stay at least one step ahead of the opposition. Finally, the high-level player needs the concentration to be able to sustain the required physical and mental output and, above all, the will to win.

2 Coaching and Teaching Volleyball

An Overview

The terms coaching and teaching are often used inter-changeably, but in reality they are very different activities. The primary difference lies in the objectives of both activities where the one, teaching, is to educate young people in terms of physical, mental, social and moral behaviour through physical activity. Whereas the coach has the objective of gaining maximum improvement in the athletes performance in keeping with their physical and mental ability and their motivation and desire to succeed. This book is primarily for coaches, although teachers may equally well use it, and for this reason the term coaching is used to describe the process of imparting information to athletes.

The coaching of volleyball, as with any other game, must be done in a realistic context, normally simulating the spatial, temporal and the type and number of opponents the player will meet in any given competitive situation. As all games are built on speed and correctness of decision-making, one of the most important aspects of the early stages of learning is that the player must work in realistic situations, which have more than one solution, thus meaning that from the outset the player has to make a decision. Only in this way will a player develop the type and speed of decision-making processes required to play COMPETITIVE VOLLEYBALL. Thus, in the early stages of coaching and teaching every player must experience every positional role, both offensive and defensive. Therefore, each player must learn to serve, receive, dig, set, spike/smash, block and cover, but NOT to play a specialised role. At this stage the rotational rule comes to the coach's assistance because it means that each player must play each role in turn.

Anticipation

Another key factor in team games is anticipation, viz. the player learns to build "models in the mind" of a number of potential outcomes from any given situation. As a result of this they are able to select the best-fit option very quickly at the appropriate time. It is very important that the coach develops understanding in the player, that is coaching so that the player understands not only what he is doing, but also what his team-mates and opponents are doing. By working in this way in the early stages of learning the coach is not only encouraging the long, sustained rallies needed for advanced play, but is also building firm foundations on which to develop the succeeding stages in the creation of the performance player, and at the same time helping the player enjoy the learning situation.

The Order of Learning

As well as developing the skill of anticipation, the order in which material is presented is equally important. In most volleyball coaching manuals the coach is given help with knowing which techniques, skills tactics and fitness training is required, but often little or no help with the timing or order in which to present them. This book provides the coach with 16 different learning outcomes presented in such a way that they cover not only the physical element of **playing skill,** but also the psycho-social aspects that develop **enjoyment and team spirit.**

What is given here is an explanation of each objective, which is dealt with in greater depth in each individual learning outcome. In the earliest stages of volleyball **the defence, receive, pass situation** is possibly the most important; in that once the players have mastered this then they will be able to keep rallies going, a factor which greatly improves **enjoyment.** Additionally, it is important, at all levels of the game, **to create a balance between the dominance of the skills of setting and spiking/smashing and the fact that a defensive move is made prior to the use of either skill.**

In terms of individual skill, players should understand from the outset that it is **the quality of defence that determines the offence!** In fact, unless the beginner understands this from the outset then his ability to keep the ball in the air may be curtailed resulting in less enjoyment. In terms of team play a team may be said to be ready to compete when their **defence is better than, or at least as good as their offence!**

Individual Playing Skill. At novice level at least a basic level of skill is very important for player enjoyment. For this reason defensive play must be given priority over offensive. In terms of the coach being able to identify when a player has achieved this outcome it is generally accepted that **when a player can consistently keep the ball in the air, i.e. volley, he is capable of playing a game.**

The following factors are important when considering the order in which to present individual, group and team tactics. The following is suggested as a possible order of presentation:

- Introducing volleyball as a moving, dynamic game, i.e. a game in which running and jumping are important.
- Improving the level of individual techniques and decision making.
- Improving each player's anticipation.
- Improving the team's communication skills.

This is best illustrated using as an example the introduction to players of how to develop an attacking move. In terms of attacking play there are differences between the individual player, the specific position of that player, for example a setter, and the situation-specific patterns of movement that he is called upon to carry out.

Player-specific pattern of movement: For the player who is playing at performance level this requires specialist knowledge of the game, and is therefore thematically only one component of the game.

Position-specific movement pattern: Means that the position specific to, let's say, the setter and his position are laid down from the start of play. This is unlike **situation-specific patterns of play.** For example, depending of the specific situation the player finds himself in he will independently decide to whom he is going to pass. Right from the start of play each player is faced with different decisions that have to be made both quickly and accurately if the outcome is to be successful. For this reason the coach should lay more emphasis on working on situation-specific play as opposed to position-specific play.

Having said this, work on **position-specific** offence early in the learning process needs to be done as it demands passing and defending skills on the part of each player. This is often very difficult for beginners to achieve and so play frequently breaks down. This is exacerbated by the fact that neither the setter nor the receiving player are ready to receive a second pass, and therefore do not respond either quickly or accurately to the pattern of play anticipating that each pass will be accurate and therefore easy to return. In fact only when the players are more accurate in their response should special patterns be introduced.

For this reason game sequences and combinations, in which the objective of first ball contact (player/position) is laid down from the start of play, are not introduced until well into the learning sequence (LO 7), when players may be expected to be able to anticipate unexpected and realistic situations and respond accordingly.

The most important elements involved in teaching volleyball are that:

- The players understand that the game includes running and jumping.
- They develop the skills of the game and make the correct situation-specific decisions.
- They develop an understanding between each team member.

As players become more adept, the 0:0:6 system of play is best used because each player should be equally experienced in all the basic situations and can play the different roles. The 0:0:6 system means that each player can play a 'utility role' being able to solve defensive, offensive and setting tasks.

As with all sport, the importance of maintaining the players interest and motivation cannot be over-stressed. This book advocates the learning by **playing the game method** to achieve this objective, which may be achieved incrementally by learning through **game-like sequences** and where safe through **drills and skills.** In other words, it is important to adopt a **synthesis of methods,** particularly with regard to **error analysis and correction.** In working on the various learning objectives proposed in this text, it is important to consider both the basic skills and frequently encountered problems. In order to make good any shortfall it may be necessary to use such as situation-specific drill involving partner work and small group work as well as game-like situations.

Learning Objectives

It should be possible to achieve a learning outcome within 2 sessions, the first providing a launch pad for the second. If the work involves a technical or tactical element which mutually affect each other then both individual and group work should be included in both sessions. As a general rule, individual tactics should be coached alongside individual skills, while group tactics should be covered during team tactic sessions. During the sessions the focus is essentially on **small-court games.** This method is advocated because it will help to train target and accuracy skills (the so-called techno-motor skills) plus it helps to build group tactics using simplified conditions (team play). It is very important to remember the acquisition of social skills and fair play. For example, in the case of a 3 : 3 situation the winning team may be the one to make most contacts, or play the longest rally or even make the least mistakes. Note that in this text players who are playing on the same side are referred to as partners, while their opponents are called team-mates. While it is very important to develop a competitive spirit in players, it is important that fair play is actively encouraged. In order to do this, learners should work with as many different partners, team-mates and opponents as possible. Only in this way will they learn to cope with the different situations and styles of play. It is also very important to move the players into a 6 : 6 situation from time to time in order to check their development in a realistic situation. Don't forget poor play on a small court will mean worse play on a full sized court. Insist on standards from the outset and do not to accept poor quality or inconsistent play.

The size of the court is not fixed rather it should be checked and if necessary changed regularly to cope with the different levels of play or incremental improvements. When selecting a court size take into account the tactical or technical element on which the players are focusing.

Remember:

1. A wide, short court will make the players move sideways and turn more, whereas a long narrow favours forward and backward motion.
2. Rule changes such as altering the height of the net, or reducing the court size can change the style of game played and may succeed in speeding up or improving the flow of the game.
3. To introduce the use of the three-touch rule as it will serve to improve player interaction.

To learn to play diagonal and parallel passes and improve peripheral vision the use of the **triangle game** is recommended, and to best place to teach this is at the net where it has the greatest real life in-game application. If using this method, take care with the delivery of the first ball in play as this will effect subsequent play.

As stated previously, this text provides 16 learning objectives. Each one follows the same pattern viz. an explanation of the method to be used, plus an overview of the proposed game form. Movements and actions are illustrated by the use of **kinegrams and cyclograms,** diagrams illustrating the movement of players on the court. Included are a series of notes and objectives to help clarify the situation also a number of **learning check-lists** to provide feedback for coach and player alike.
The ability to read the game provides players with early recognition of opponent's intentions. It is therefore vital to use such as question and answer sessions to check knowledge and correct player's analysis of any given situation. This is also a useful method of encouraging coach/player interaction. Finally at the end of each session the coach is given a list of the most common errors and ideas of corrections.

3 Hints and Tips on Potential Problems when Coaching Volleyball

As with the section Error Analysis/Corrections this chapter provides some potential problems and suggested solutions for the coach to apply within his sessions. This chapter includes problems that may arise at both beginner and more advanced levels of the game.

1. Differences in Player's Skill Levels

Suggested Solutions:
- Set up mixed ability groups with players of different skill levels.
- The coach or a skilled player plays the 'key' shot (for example a set).
- Put conditions on the better players (for example, no faking).
- Set up small-court games with different numbers of players (1:2/2:3/2:4/2:6/ 3:6 and so on).
- Adjust the height of the net for players of different skill levels. (See also under suggested solutions to point 6).

2. Too Short Rallies and Sequences of Play that are Too Short

Suggested Solutions:
- Smaller courts
- Smaller courts plus higher net
- Makes offence easier by applying different rules, for example, a gentle underarm service from a nearer position or attacks only on third contact.
- Allow double play or even a catch to help less skilful players.
- See also suggestions provided in 1 above.

3. Reduced Coaching Activity

Suggested Solutions:
- Use additional game-specific exercises, particularly small-court games, for example, players rotate 1 place after successfully getting the ball over the net, or run to behind the base or side line between each attempt.
- Check the composition of teams and ensure a balance of abilities while doing such as using a new line-up or rotational order.
- Organise small-court tournaments.
- See suggestions for 2 above.

4. Players Loosing Interest in Volleyball

Suggested Solutions:
- Organise intra- and inter-school/club tournaments.
- Visit higher level games, particularly with students using observation check list.
- Use video and analyse the players and other teams' performances.
- Try using a variety of motivational techniques such as background music, video etc.
- Use different forms of volleyball, for example volley tennis, volley basketball or mixed volleyball.
- Temporarily switch to playing another sport.
- See suggestions for 3 above.

5. Inadequate Equipment Available

Suggested Solutions:
- Improvise by using a rope hung with coloured ribbons for safety as a substitute for the net.
- Use a variety of other balls for example foam balls, hand balls or gymnastic balls.
- Use small-game situations such as where the players change functions by changing with places each other, for example, triangle game using 4/5 players only.
- Small-court and team games such as those described below:
- Form 2 groups of players and give them parallel training in different sports.

a) Make a Mistake and Leave the Court

Team structure: 2-3 teams of equal numbers on both sides of the net.

Rules:

1. Only one team each is playing (see Fig. 3).
2. As soon as a team makes a mistake they quickly leave the court and are replaced by the next team who are waiting behind the base line. This new group gets to put the ball into play (either by a serve or a throw).
3. The positional roles of each player will change each time a different player serves the ball.
4. The winners are the first team to win a set or reach a predefined number of points.
5. Points are scored whenever the opponents make a mistake.

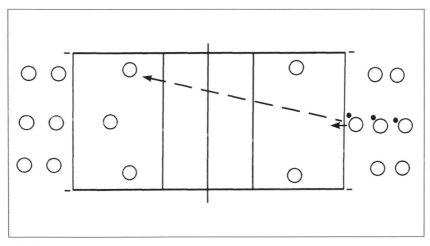

Fig. 3

b) Travelling Change

Rules:

1. The teams change as above but this time only when the ball crosses the net.
2. Teams consists of six players on court with an additional three to six players waiting to come on court (see Fig. 4).
3. 3 ball contacts are compulsory.
4. The changes and points are as in the game above, but on each change the group of forward players (A) is replaced by a group of back players (B) and as appropriate by the placement players (C) or by players waiting off court.

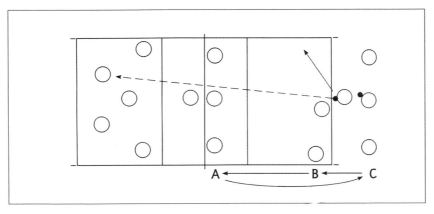

Fig. 4

6. Problems in Coaching Mixed/Co-educational Groups

Suggested Solutions:
When playing mixed volleyball, female players (F) should be allowed to play at positions III/IV/V on the left hand side of the playing court, and positions I/II/VI on the right hand side of the court, with the male players taking up the other positions. It is also important to modify the changeovers, for example the women and men rotate separately, and such that each player will play in each position in turn.

* It is suggested that the coach uses different game patterns, for example, small-court games and using a sloping net. N.B. always check that female players play on the lower end of the net (see Fig. 5).

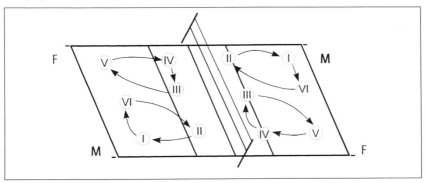

Fig. 5

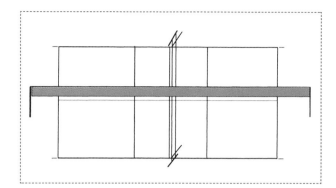

Fig. 7
Net divider

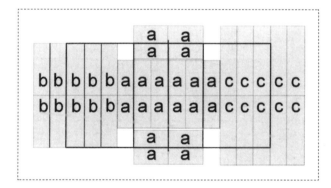

Fig. 8
A =1.5 x 3m
B = 2.25 x 4.5m
C = 2.25 x 6m

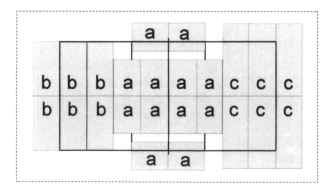

Fig. 9
A = 2.25 x 3m
B = 1.5 x 4.5m
C = 1.5 x 6m

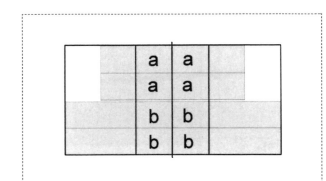

Fig. 10
A = 2.25 x 6m
B = 2.25 x 9m

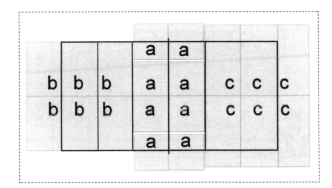

Fig. 11
A = 3 x 3m
B = 3 x 4.5m
C = 3 x 6m

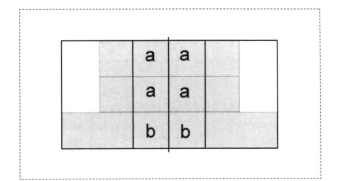

Fig. 12
A = 3 x 6m
B = 3 X 9m

4 Coaching Mini-Volleyball

The aim of this chapter is to explain the 'philosophy' that underpins this book and to provide the coach with an insight into the training of mini-volleyball. It also provides practical advice on how to coach, plus ideas of the type and amount of information that should be included for any given level of ability.

The author's philosophy is to let young players have as much fun as possible while learning, and to always work in as realistic and game-like situations/setting as possible. It is felt that **mini-volleyball and small-court games** provide the basic building blocks for the development of the future performance player. The basic skills of the game and patterns of play are both learnt through these games which are all volleyball-specific in terms of space, time, target, partners and opponents. Indeed, if coached well in the early stages, the transfer to competitive volleyball should be relatively straightforward.

It is essential that the teaching of the basic technical elements such as the volley and dig pass, roll shot and underarm service is done in a game-like manner making it as much fun as possible. In terms of tactics they should be taught such that it will occur spontaneously in a game, especially the group and individual tactical behaviour.

It is recommended that the ideal age to start to play mini-volleyball is about 10 years, although it will depend on the physical and intellectual development of the individual as to the precise age to begin. However, it is important to remember that at primary level all children should be exposed to a variety of sports and activities. Indeed previous exposure to games that involve such skills as catching, throwing, bouncing, rolling and hitting should make a contribution to learning the game of volleyball. Minor games that are based on such objectives as "ball onto opponent's area" and "ball over the net" makes an ideal introduction to volleyball. By introducing volleyball at this age and to children with this type of background means that they should be competent mini-volleyball players in 2-3 years.

The first skills that should be introduced are the volley and dig pass, which should be introduced virtually in order to get the game started, and to introduce children to the decision-making process. The use of skills in digging and setting increases the playing of rallies by reason of the fact that radius of action is bigger, so more balls can be reached, and digging gives younger players more confidence because their hands may be too small for the balls. Adding one-handed actions with regard to techniques such as set should support this and dig passes.

REMEMBER! As a general rule the following principle should always be observed "**two-handed passes always take precedence over those using one hand and volley passes have precedence over dig passes.**"

The introduction of the technique of serving advocated by many authors does not, in the opinion of the authors of his book, prove satisfactory in that it leads to too many errors and breakdowns in play very early in the game. In order to avoid these interruptions and to get a game started as quickly as possible use such as a throw or even use a simple volley pass to get the ball into play. The underarm service should be taught towards the end of the course. More important than serving is the introduction of jumping actions such as one or both arm swings, with hitting over the net. The jumping actions should start the spiking/smashing from a standing position to a roll shot in the air. By working in this way the player will be using a two-footed instead of a one-foot take-off.

In parallel with techniques and skills the coach must introduce tactics. For example, service, receiving and defending will be the first tactics to be covered, by one to two-man units, followed by three to four-man units. Offensive play will initially be situation-specific, and only later will it become position-specific.

REMEMBER! "**Play high rather than low and further away from rather than close to the net!**"

The Game

It is very important to introduce the game developmentally and for this reason the 1:1 game should be the first one played. This may be collaborative as well as competitive. As the players become more adept it will be important to introduce 2:2, 3:3 and 4:4 games, which will naturally include the tactics of attack and defence.

REMEMBER! Communication between players is a vitally important aspect of tactical training and the following should always apply "**the first person to move or call, plays the ball**".

REMEMBER! The aim of introducing basic techniques and basic tactics is to **introduce the game of volleyball in a complete and fun way** such that the youngsters will enjoy the game and hence be motivated to continue.

Techniques

1. **Setting or Volley Pass**
- Stress the body/ball relationship: 'player under/behind the ball'.
- Point of contact 'play the ball using ALL the fingers'.
- Impetus: 'whole body extension'.

2. **Dig Pass**
- Body/ball relationship ' player BEHIND ball'.
- Point of contact: 'play the ball with both forearms extended and hands together'.
- Impetus: 'whole body extension'.

3. **Roll Shot/Drive**
- Positioning: 'jump under the ball using a two-footed take-off'.
- Impetus: 'arms fully extended'.
- Point of contact: 'hit the ball with the hand'.

4. **Underarm Serve**
- Impetus 'arm swings parallel to the body'.
- Point of contact body/ball relationship: 'hit the ball, which is fed in low, with the hand from a point behind and below'.

Tactics

1. **Game 1:1**
- Select a reception and defence position such that 2/3rds of the court can be covered after the player moves forward.
- If possible, have the player play from a standing position.
- If playing collaboratively, hit the ball towards the partner, if playing competitively, hit the ball away from the opponent.

2. **Game 2:2**
- Early communication with partner.
- At least 2 ball contacts.
- First pass high and diagonal and not too close to the net; second pass high and parallel and not too close to the net.

- When playing competitively, play the last ball away from or right between the opponent while jumping.

3. Game 3:3
- All players must be ready for the 1st, 2nd and 3rd ball contact.
- Use the 3rd ball as an offensive shot against the opponent.
- After the ball has crossed the net, take up a defensive position as quickly as possible.

4. Game 4:4
- Watch and anticipate the movements of team-mates and opponents alike.
- Speedy understanding and appreciation of the current game situation, and game-oriented use of techniques.
- Speedy understanding and appreciation of game-oriented group tactical patterns in receiving/defending, setting/attacking.

The rational transition point from mini-volleyball player to an all-around player will depend on the following 2 prerequisites:

- The players' ability to reproduce the basic skills, especially the dive, accurately and consistently.
- The players' ability to read the game tactically, particularly situation-orientated offence from the 3 and 4 passing unit.

4. Training Mental Tenacity

The new system has also increased the importance of mental skills. Error prevention has become even more significant, particularly in top-level high-pressure matches. If servers do not deliver their serves properly because they are afraid of making errors, they will soon find the ball travelling all over the place and themselves powerless to do anything about it. Many will experience the same things that players experienced ten years ago following the introduction of the tiebreak. At first everybody will feel under intense pressure, but after a while, players will grow accustomed to it. After the initial pressure, the pendulum will return to normality. We do think, however, that a high psychological level will be reached at top levels at least.

Training must now involve more stress training as psychological training must be improved. Psycho-regulative measures for monitoring stress should be taught and be able to be used.

5. Emphasizing Stress Training

Training must be adapted to the new situation. It must be turned into psychologically managed stress training. In the past we used tiebreak games to increase mental strain in training, from now on complex exercises with concrete tasks must be implemented. For instance, a single serve or serve-taking action must be carried out five times consecutively without errors, otherwise the player must start again. This type of training is required in order to prevent errors from occurring in stress situations, yet still train at a high technical and tactical level. In the final analysis, training must be adapted to the increased mental strain to that expected during games. Always train one time more than previously under mental pressure (stress training and psycho-regulation are very important). Now the training principles leading to mental pressure should be applied more than ever, i.e. if possible, all players should be trained to become point-ball players. If a team previously had one or two point-ball players, it should now have at least three or four of them.

6. Train the New Rhythm

People used to say that a set only really got going when ten points had been scored. That is no longer the case. The very first point can help decide a set because it has become difficult to make up a large lead. For this reason there will be no more casual warming up period. This phase when teams first adjust to the set before really getting going is a thing of the past. In future players will have to warm up properly before the game, and teachers and coaches will have to make sure in the breaks that players give their all, right from the start. Everyone must adapt to the new situation in training. Full concentration from the first moment onwards. Short but more intensive training sessions will be necessary.

At least two systems of play must be trained, one with the libero and at least one more without the libero, in order to be prepared for all possible situations. Players must also be trained for the new pattern of breaks in matches, i.e. for the technical timeouts and the ten minute breaks after the second and fourth sets. These new breaks must be simulated in training. So a one minute break should be taken between exercises or a ten minute break with a brief discussion, where absolute attention must be paid to maintaining tension. The breaks must not lead to an interruption of the playing rhythm, the players must stay mentally and athletically "warm", i.e. training blocks and exertion must be adapted to the new time structure of the game!

The total amount of training, however, will not be reduced as in volleyball precise actions and optimum cooperation of the players on the small court are paramount

7. Use all Options on the Bench and the Sidelines

The fact that all ball exchanges now count makes it more important than ever that all the options provided by the players are put to use. This means that coaches must exploit all the special skills of the players at the sidelines. We can only advise all coaches to use all six changes if they have the people: a good server in pos. I, brief deployment of block experts at the net and above all the employment of wingers because they do not use up the allowed changes. Additionally the coaches now has more influencing options as a result of freedom of movement so that during games he can now act the same way as in training.

8. Taking Timeouts Earlier

Coaches also have to take timeouts earlier than before. Three points in succession now constitute a more serious handicap than previously. An early lead by the opponent greatly increases the risk of losing a set. Therefore coaches must attempt to influence the match as early as possible from the outside. In order to give the players much better information, coaches need to make use of all opportunities for coaching from the sideline, for this corresponds exactly to the training situation. Player and game observation and the team's adjustment to the opponent take on considerably more significance.

Learning Objective 1:

The Forward Volley and Dig Pass

Situational Analysis

Based on the skills of volleying, digging and setting acquired in mini-volleyball, this chapter will deal with the **use and importance of volley passing** in the context of receiving and second ball defensive passing, and the introduction of an offensive progression. At this stage it is important to emphasise the necessity to achieve an acceptable level of skill in the dig and the volley, although offensive moves at this stage do not usually require high skill levels in the forearm dig. Through training and coach observation the necessary decision making skills will be acquired. These should be worked upon firstly using a small court, and only later applying within the full game. In this way it is anticipated that the players will improve their skill levels both in the movement to the ball and also after turning the body before setting the ball (see Fig. 22 below).

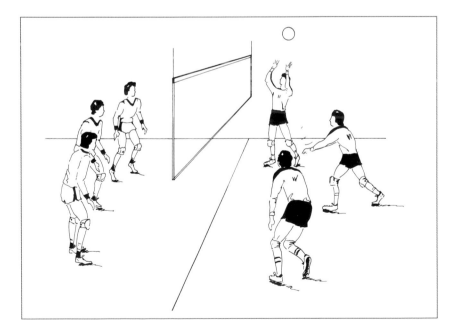

Fig. 22

Session 1: The Forward Volley Pass

Action Sequence (Fig. 23)

Fig. 23

As shown above the player moves from a half bent "ready position" to the setting place using quick, short steps. All movements to the ball including body turn (i.e. running turn – stand – play) **MUST** be finished before the player makes contact with the ball (see Fig. 24).

When the ball is contacted, the player is **under and behind the ball with knees bent,** the feet are hip-width apart, one leg ahead of the other. The weight is predominantly on the balls of the feet; the arms and legs are slightly bent while the trunk is straight. Before making contact with the ball the **whole body extends** quickly to meet the ball.

Fig. 24

Observation Points:
- Is the player able to watch both the opponent and the ball?
- In pressure situations do the players volley high to the opponents in order to gain time?
- Is the opponent observed prior to ball contact in order to help anticipation of the flight path of the ball?
- Is the opponent observed prior to the player's ball contact in order to be able to play the return pass as far from him as possible?

Game Form 1.5

Game structure: 3 : 3
Court size: 4.5 x 4.5m (see Fig. 13 b), later 4.5 x 6m (see Figs. 13 a and 14 c)
Rules:
1. The ball is tossed into play.
2. The 1st ball is either dug or volleyed into play, the 2nd and 3rd MUST be volleyed.
3. The duration of the game is 5-8 minutes.
4. The rules of the full game apply (see Fig. 32 above).

Coaching Points:
- Always execute the 1st ball contact DIAGONAL to the net and the 2nd PARALLEL to the net.
- As in game 5 above, but three ball contacts must be made.
- As game 5 above, but only volley passes are allowed.

Observation Points:
- Of the two possible setting positions does the player chose the one which gives the highest percentage chance of success and which can be executed with greatest accuracy?
- Is it possible for the team to attack after setting?
- Have the team understood that a volley pass will help them to go on the offensive?

Game Form 1.6

Game structure: 2 : 2
Court size: 4.5 x 4.5m (see Fig. 13 b) and later 4.5 x 6m (see Figs. 13 c and 14 a)
Objective: Play the game as 5 above and with variations (see Fig. 33).

Learning Check-List
- Can all players volley the ball continuously for 30 seconds without the skill breaking down using a target (3m high and 1.5m wide) on the wall?
- Can the players volley the ball more than 10 times without a break to a target (3m high and 0.5m diameter)?

Errors and Corrections – Volleying

! **Errors in the Basic Position**
- The players play the ball while in motion rather than from a safe static position.
- The players adopt a straddle position instead of one leg ahead of the other.
- The weight is on the heels as opposed to the balls of the feet.
- The weight is placed on one side as opposed to equally balanced between the two feet.

Suggested Solutions:
- Exercises without the ball or holding the ball; on the whistle stop, assume the ready position and play the ball.
- Exercises with the ball thrown, later volleyed and played. It is important for the players to observe and correct each other.
- Working with a partner and later in groups of three, play balls that are thrown and then volleyed with different degrees of accuracy and height. For example:
  a) Throw/volley the ball high and forwards, next play the ball high to player B who must set back accurately.
  b) As above, but initially in pairs and finally in a triangle, with very acute angles.

! **Errors in Co-ordination**
- Only using the arms and legs instead of extending the whole body.
- Using extended rather than bent arms before contacting the ball.
- Poor timing of the full body extension, i.e. extending too early or too late.
- Wrist action directed forwards instead of upwards.
- Elbows out to the side instead of forwards and outwards.

Suggested Solutions:
- Simulate the setting position, and from a low position throw medicine balls.
- Practice setting the ball, alternating high and low.
- Using a low position, for example sitting on a box or bench, set the ball high towards a target.

Session 2: The Frontal Dig Set

Action Sequence (see Fig. 35)

In the case of the frontal set the player moves the same way as for a normal set, i.e. with quick, short steps towards the receiving point. It is very important that on making contact the player is still.

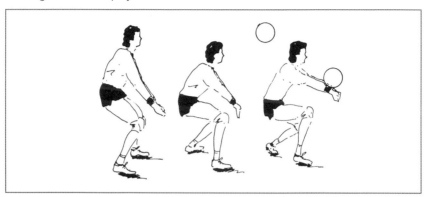

Fig. 35

Once having received the ball, the player is **behind the ball with one leg ahead of the other** about a foot to half a foot length in distance, the weight is mainly over the balls of the feet, which are hip-width apart. The legs are slightly bent and the trunk is bent forwards with the arms extended and the hands turned palm upwards with the hands laid in each other. By bending the wrists and pushing the shoulders forwards the arms are extended such that the forearms are held together with their wide inner surface forming the contact point (see Fig. 36).

Shortly before ball contact there is a strong **extension of the whole body** and the ball is contacted by the forearms at hip level. The player ends the movement after the dig, the **arms do not rise above shoulder level** and the player is able to resume the "ready position".

Fig. 36

N.B. As a general rule the lower the ball flies, the lower the ready position; the faster the ball, the less the arms and legs extend.

When the player has mastered this shot, the next in sequence is the forearm dig, with the objective of making the transition from dig set to forearm dig as smooth as possible.

Explanation

The aim of the opposing team is to play the ball directly at the floor, to areas of the court that are not covered, or to empty zones. This makes dig setting an essential defensive action. At this stage in player development the offensive skills are not well developed and therefore all high flying balls should be received with a dig set to pass. It is important that the player should take up position behind the ball and try to play it while facing forwards. The test of the quality of the first ball contact is the possibility of rolling the volley pass with the second ball contact.

Game Form 2.1

Game structure: 2 : 2 (see Fig. 37)

Fig. 37

Court size: 4.5 x 4.5m (see Fig. 13 b)
Objective: Players should experience the 2-handed dig set as the most appropriate travelling technique to receive slow and low balls, and pass the ball high and accurately to a forward zone in order to make a volley set from a standing position.
Rules:
1. Time 3-5 minutes.
2. The players' pass to each other using a dig set.

Game Form 2.2

Game Structure: 3:3 (see Fig. 39)
Court size: 4.5 x 4.5m (see Fig. 13 b), later 4.5 x 6m (see Fig. 13 c/14 a)
Rules:

1. All general rules apply plus the following special rules.
2. At least two ball contacts must be made by both sides. In order to achieve this, it may be necessary to start play by using either an underarm serve or volley set.
3. As above, but three ball contact must be made.
4. As above, but with additional tasks such as after the ball passes over the net the player must run and touch the side line, and later base line. The attacking build-up is executed by frontcourt or backcourt players.

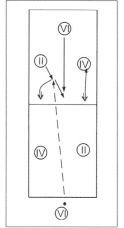

Fig. 39

Coaching Points:

- Try to always keep both the ball and the opponent in sight.
- Try to anticipate your opponent's intentions from his position in relation to the ball.
- Bear in mind that you can move faster forwards than backwards, so select a starting position such that you have 2/3rds of the defence area in front of you with only 1/3rd to the rear.
- The player who moves to the ball first should play it.
- Make your intentions clear by clearly calling "mine" or "me".

Game Form 2.3

Game Structure: 2:2
Court size: 3 x 4.5m (see Fig. 11 b), later 4.5 x 4.5m (see Fig. 13 b)
Rules: as above (see also Figs. 33 and 37 above)

Game Form 2.4

Game Structure: 1:1
Court size: 2.25 x 4.5m (see Fig. 9), later 3 x 4,5m (see Fig. 11 b) and 3 x 6m (see Figs. 11 c/12 a)
Rules: 3 successive ball contacts allowed. Otherwise general rules apply.

Game Form 2.5

Mini-Volleyball Game (See Fig. 39)
Court size: 4.5 x 6m, (see Figs. 13 c/14 a)
Same as game 2:2 above.

Observation Points:

- Do the players understand when to use a dig set or is this shot used even in circumstances when a volley set would be possible?
- Do the players appreciate the importance of the triangle formation as the basic volleyball formation?

Learning Check-List:

- Working for 30 seconds can all players toss the ball over a wall marking placed at 3 metres height?
- Can all players toss the ball accurately more than 10 times to hit a target marked 3 x 1m in diameter marked on a wall?
- Can all players play a dig set more than 20 times in succession using a circle of diameter 3 metres?

Errors/Corrections of the Front Dig Set

! Errors in the Basic Position

- The ball is played while moving and not from a static position.
- A straddle position is used instead of one foot in front of the other.
- Weight on the heels as opposed to the balls of the feet.
- Legs extended as opposed to bent.

Suggested Solutions:

- See session 1 regarding the volley set which may also be used here.

! Errors in Impetus and/or Co-ordination

- Impetus being obtained mainly from the arms instead of the legs.
- Ball played with arms bent instead of straight.
- Body extension only takes place when or after contact is made with the ball instead of slightly before the ball is hit.
- The body is extended too early in the action, such that the dig is executed at shoulder height as opposed to hip level.

Suggested Solutions:

- Use drills in which the player, from a low ready position, digs the stationary thrown or volleyed ball.
- Work with the player holding a ball between the arms and upper chest while carrying out a dig pass.
- The player touches the floor with both hands before each reception of he ball.

variety of attacks, require and assist a generally applicable development as **all the players** must be prepared to play any role, and the different game situations will decide who takes responsibility. The use of situational offence should serve to challenge the cognitive ability of a player (see Teaching Concept).

Session 1: The Underarm Serve

Action Sequence (Fig. 41)

Fig. 41

- The serve is played with the feet shoulder-width apart in a front to back position, with both feet pointing to the net; for right-handed players the front foot is the left one.
- The legs are slightly bent.
- The ball is held in the left hand in front of the body at hip level.
- The serving arm, i.e. the left, is taken directly back, the weight is placed on the back foot and then the arm swings forwards like a pendulum.
- The ball may be tossed up slightly or dropped directly prior to contact.
- Contact is made with the palm of the hand from behind/below at hip level at about an arm's length in front of the body.
- The hand is tensed and takes on the 'shape' of the ball.
- The stretching of the legs is coupled with the serving action, which causes the body weight to shift to the front foot.

Explanation

The Serving Team
The ball is brought into play by the serve, which has the objective of either gaining a point directly, or putting the opposition under so much pressure that they find it difficult to attack. It is therefore very important to be able to serve

safely and accurately. Ideal targets for a serve are a weak player, a space between the receiving players or poorly covered zones.

The Receiving Team

For the receiving team anticipation is very important as it is vital to pick up cues regarding such as the flight path and direction of the ball as early as possible. Based upon this information it will be possible to select the correct counter-attacking move. The receiving team's ability to do this to a very large extent depends on the quality of the original service.

Game Form 1.1 (see Fig. 42)

Game structure: 1:2
Court size: 4.5 x 6m (see Fig. 13 c⁄14)
Objective:
The aim of this practice is to remind players of the importance of the underarm serve, which can be both accurate, very effective and can be used as the first attack
Rules:
1. The serving player has 5 or 10 serves.
2. The 2 receiving players take up position using the 2-player pattern (2 man passing unit) and pass the ball using 3 contacts over the net into the opponent's court such that the server cannot return it.

Fig. 42

3. After this the 3 players change position and roles.
4. Only the server can win points by:
    a) directly winning from a service ace
    b) if the opposition cannot make 3 consecutive ball contacts
    c) If he can play the returned ball either with a volley or a dig set.
5. The winner is the server who wins most points in 2-3 sets.

Playing Tips

a) Avoid errors in the execution of the serve (safety is more important than a risky serve) by serving from the centre of the service area.
b) Stand in the step position facing the net.

Games and Variations in Changed Formation of the 6-Player Pattern (see Fig. 52 a-c)

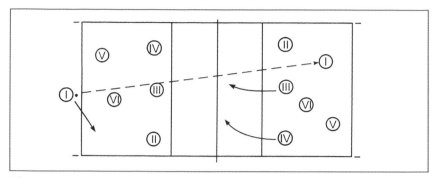

Fig. 52 a

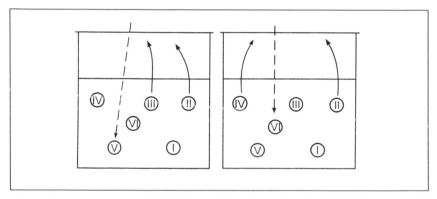

Fig. 52 b / c

Observation Check-List

- Because there are errors in setting is it necessary to refer back to Lesson 1/LO 1?
- Is it understood that the server serves on the strengths and weaknesses of the opponent?
- Do the players have great difficulties in receiving the serve?
- Do the players behave as required by a given situation, i.e. do they move to the setting area at the net if not receiving the serve?
- Can it be judged that the server commits fewer errors if serving from the middle of the serving area?

Learning Check-List:
The players can correctly answer test questions (if necessary with the help of sketches) concerning:
- The two line-up possibilities and employment of the 6-player pattern.
- The defence areas and responsibilities of the players, especially of the front-court players.
- Free play observation of the 6-player pattern.

Errors/Corrections of the 6-Player Pattern

- Players stand behind each other instead of in gaps, thus allowing eye contact to the server.
- Reception areas are not clear owing to the incorrect line-up.
- The forward players stand too close to the net instead of 1-2m behind the attack line and are more ready to play setting than receiving.
- The player in position III stands in the middle of the court instead of positioning himself left or right according to the line-up (see Figs. 47 and 48).

Suggested Solutions:
- Revisit theoretical education on the line-up and responsibilities of the receiving players.
- With the help of different aids (drawings, pictures, video-recordings, markings on the court to help orientation etc.).
- Train the use of the pattern without the ball through rotation on command, quick take-up of the line-up, and checking and if necessary correct.

! Errors in the Attack via Forward Players
- Forward players acting as setters start too early or too late towards the net instead of at the moment when the direction of the serve is clearly recognizable.
- Setters move to the attacking zone without keeping an eye on the ball.
- Receiving players do not decide in time where to pass the ball.
- Reception pass is executed vertically, as opposed to diagonally to the net.

Suggested Solutions:
- Practice exercises in which the ball, initially thrown or passed, later hit, is received in the 6-player pattern. First the direction of the serve and the kind of attack are determined, and the different attack patterns via forward players are repeatedly exercised/practiced.

6. After 24 drives the 4-player groups will change roles.
7. The winner is the 4-player group with the most points in one or two sets.

Coaching Points:
- In the case of high and slowly moving balls the attack will run via the forward-court player on the forward court, in the case of low and fast moving balls via the backcourt player with the second pass from the backcourt.
- Volley the easy drives diagonally to the forward court, to dig the difficult balls high to the middle of the court.
- Save high and slowly travelling balls with volley set, in order to pass more accurately (double contact is not breaking the rules in this case).
- As a backcourt player also be prepared to take over the set from the back court when partners play defence.

Variations on Game Form 2.1

1. Drive from position II.
2. Drive changing from position II and IV (see Fig. 66 b).

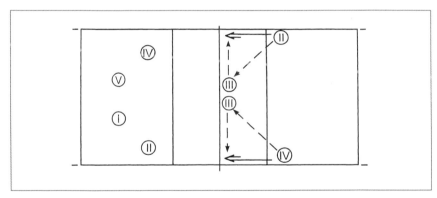

Fig. 66 b

Game Form 2.2

Game structure 4:4
Court size: 6 x 9m (see Fig. 16 b)
Rules:
According to the game rules but with a special rule that every ball over the net must be directed or hit to the backcourt. The defence without block takes place similar to 4-player pattern (see Fig. 60).

Variations on Game Form 2.2

1. **Game structure:** 5:5
   Rules: The defence without block takes place in a kind of 5-player pattern (see Fig. 61).
2. As Game Form 2.2 and variation (1), but on a playing field of 9 x 9m (see Fig. 6).
3. Same as above, but the attack can also be played on the forward court.

Coaching Points:
- Watch setters and attackers in order to recognize the direction of the ball and the place of the defence early.
- Let your team-mates know your intentions (calling out).
- In the case of attack from the backcourt, play the first pass so high that the second pass can be set overhead.
- Play the second pass from the backcourt diagonally high and not too close to the net.
- As an attacker, always adjust the starting position to the kind of attack action, by running from outside diagonally to the net, when there is a set from the backcourt.

Game Form 2.3

Game structure: 6:6
Court size: 9 x 9m (see Fig. 6)
Rules:
According to the game rules with a special rule that the team receives an additional point for each successful drive after defence without blocking (see Figs. 63/64).

Observation Points:
- Is it necessary to refer to EE of Session 2 because of difficulties already in the game form in the transition from defence to attack?
- Does the attack action with the second pass from the backcourt increase the effectiveness of play? *
- Is it certain that the players understand and execute both patterns to start the attack from defence and play according to the situation?
- Are there breaks in the game because the players misjudge the defence situation?
- Is it necessary to train the diagonal pass separately?
- Is it necessary to refer to Session 1 because of major problems in executing the drive?

! **Errors in Teamwork between Defenders/Receivers and Setters, and between Receivers, Setters and Attackers**

- Difficulties and misunderstandings among the players due to lack of readiness and insufficient communication.
- Lack of readiness to carry out the first, second or third ball contact.
- In the case of a pass from the backcourt the attacker does not choose the place and direction of the approach at the correct angle to the ball trajectory.

Suggested Solution:

- Renewed discussion of the types of attack under consideration of the various communicating principles (see Session 2 under LO 2).

Further Response Rules:

- Players moving forwards to the ball as receiver, setter or attacker, have priority over players moving backwards to the ball.
- In the case of setting between attackers, the player with his hitting arm near the ball should hit it.
- When passing between setters, the player who has to turn his body the least to execute the diagonal pass should play the ball.
- See the aforementioned drills in connection with attack whereby the passes are deliberately played to the overlaps in the areas of responsibility of receivers, setters or attackers.
- Choose the starting position of the attacker appropriate to the situation and use drills that are suitable. Sets are executed first from the same place, later from changing positions from the backcourt. Additionally, drills in which attack situations via forward-court players and backcourt players alternate. Start with one attacker, then later with 2 or 3 attackers.

Learning Objective 4:

Jump Set Sideways/Reverse Set 6-Player Pattern with Attack via Backcourt Players

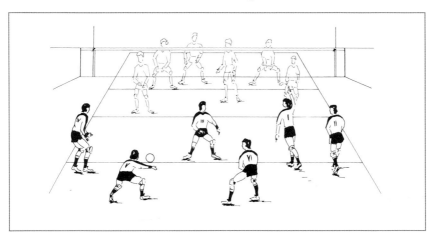

Fig. 71

Situational Analysis

Attacking via the backcourt players means that one of the back players runs to the forward court in order to take the responsibility for setting. In this chapter this will first be taught and trained as **free running from the 6-player pattern**. The attack via the back players is an additional variation to the types of attack used so far (via forward-court player and second pass from backcourt) and should improve the tactical understanding of backcourt players.

To carry out free running play with back players from the 6-player pattern (see Session 3) an important prerequisite is the ability of the players to execute volley and dig sets with variety and accuracy. Sessions 1 and 2 therefore deal with the improvement of volley and dig setting.

Dig setting from the side (side dig set), as explained in Session 1, is used in game situations when it is not possible for the player to take up position facing the ball. Such situations, and the need to be successful, create the need to use the drive in particular, The side dig set, both at the introduction of the attack from reception (dig set) as well as from defence (forearm dig), are therefore referred to again in Session 3.

Learning Check-List
See "Learning Check" for frontal dig set (LO 1/Session 2).

Errors/Corrections of the Side Dig Set

! **Errors in the Basic Position**
- The ball is played while moving instead of from a standing position.
- Missing the fencing step, or the fencing step is done with the leg further from the ball, not with the leg nearest to the ball.

Suggested Solutions:
- Work on partner exercises where the ball is first thrown/played, and then later softly hit exactly to the side of the practicing player.
- At the beginning, the direction and flight of the ball are determined in advance and are constant; later both are varied. It is important that the ball moves at hip level and the distance between player/ball, and also partner/ball is gradually increased (see Figs. 75 a/b).
- Small-court game against each other on a wide rather than long playing field if possible, in order to force the execution of the side dig set.

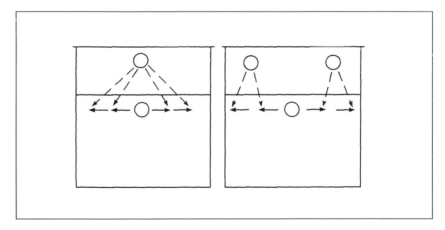

Figs. 75 a/b

! **Errors in Body-ball-relationship**
- The ball is played at shoulder level instead of hip level with arms turned up.
- The ball is played only from below or behind instead of from behind and below.

Suggested Solutions:

All the above drills are concerned with the height and direction of the ball trajectory. Play is directed to a target (basketball hoop/board on the wall, goal hoops, etc.) above a given rope, but the setting direction is opposite to the direction of the movement (see Figs. 76 a/b).

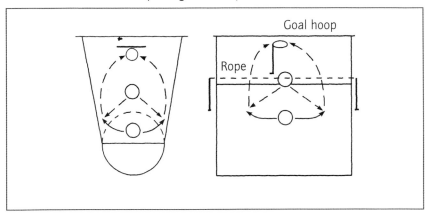

Figs. 76 a/b

See also EE of Session 2/LO 1.

Game Form 2.4

Game structure: 4:4
Court size: 6 x 6m, later 9 x 6m
Rules:
1. The positions II/III/IV and VI are taken up.
2. Position I acts as setter, reception is in 3-player pattern (Fig. 85).
3. Follow game rules with some specific rules viz. an additional point is given for each successful drive after a reverse set

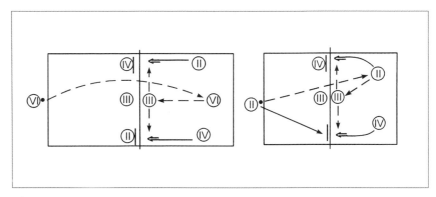

Fig. 85   *Fig. 86*

Variation on Game Form 2.4

Game structure: 3:3
Court size: 6 x 4.5m, later 9 x 4.5m
Rules:
The positions I/II/IV are taken up; reception in two player pattern (see Fig. 86).

Coaching Points:
- Do the players stand below and behind the ball in the case of a front volley and below the ball in the case of a reverse set?
- Are legs and arms extended in the same direction?
- Does the set cause misunderstandings and difficulties in setter/attacker teamwork?
- Does the dig set action need to be further improved in order to execute the pass to the setter more accurately and safely?
- Does the attack from a prescribed position cause difficulties?

Learning Check-List:
- Can each player reverse-volley at least three times out of ten into a goal hoop 3m away?
- The hoop is placed horizontally in position II at a height of III m and has a maximum diameter of 1m. The player is in position III and throws the ball to himself for hitting (see Fig. 87).

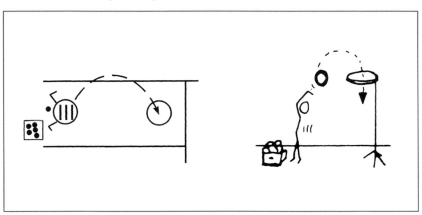

Fig. 87

Errors/Corrections of the Reverse Set

Because of the similarity in the movements of the front and reverse set the drills of LO 1/Session 1 can be applied; nevertheless, at the moment of ball contact the changed body-ball-relationship must be considered.

! **Errors in the Body-ball-relationship**
- At the moment of ball contact the player stands behind/below instead of below the ball.
- The player stretches upwards and forwards instead of upwards and backwards in the extension of the body axis.
- The arms are extended backwards with exaggerated arching instead of backwards and upwards with the upper body straight.
- The player takes the ball in front of the body instead of standing under the ball.
- The player no longer watches the ball at the moment of contact instead of keeping his eye on it as long as possible.

Suggested Solutions:
- Exercises in which the ball is hit high.
- Same as before, but going backwards slightly.
- Drills where the balls first thrown by the player, later accurately volleyed, are played backwards.
- Drills where the high, but inaccurately thrown/volleyed balls, are played backwards to the partner, later to targets (e.g. target on the wall, basketball ring, goal hoop, etc.).
- Drills where the player has to play the ball, which he throws to her/himself from a sitting position over a high marking behind him.
- Drills - same as above - but from a standing position, later after a preceding movement with the execution of a reverse set..

! **Errors in Setting Accuracy**
- The ball is played away from the line of the body's axis.
- The player passes while moving or turning, instead of from a safe standing position.
- The player passes in fencing step position instead of straddle position.

Suggested Solutions:
- Exercises in groups of three with series of passes via the middle player.
- The groups of three stand parallel to the net/wall/line, i.e. orientation aids, (see Fig. 79).
- See also previous drills, primarily those directed to targets.

Session 3: 6-Player Pattern with Offence via Backcourt Players

Action Sequence

The line-up possibilities, defence areas and the players' responsibilities when receiving serves in 6-player pattern are the same as those in LO 2/Session 2 (see Figs. 46/47/48). This also applies to the **principles of free running** where the direction of the serve determines the setting area and also the setter, and play is with a diagonal first pass and a parallel second pass.

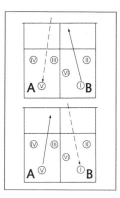

In the case of an **attack via backcourt players from the 6-player pattern** all the players should be involved in the reception and the pass of the serve. The backcourt players, who stand the furthest away from each other in the line-up (see Fig. 88 a/b), initially assume the role of setters. When the serve is received by one of the players in court A, the backcourt player I as setter will run to the forward court

Fig. 88 a/b

zone between positions II and III directly after the serve has been executed and the direction of the serve identified (see Fig. 88 a/b). Similarly the backcourt player V acts as setter between position III and IV if the ball is served to court 'B'. Despite the longer distance compared to offence via forward-court players, the setter **(runner)** tries to reach the setting position before the serve is received in order to make the type and location of the planned offence clear. The diagonal first pass makes setting parallel to the net easier for the runner. The main aim of this running play is to use all the three players at the net as attackers.

Explanation

In the 6-player pattern all players are involved in service reception. Depending on the line-up, the backcourt players will take over setting to the forward zone in pairs V, V, V, I and V, I and IV or V and VI (free running). When attacking with backcourt players V, and I if the players in positions IV/V and III have to receive, player I acts as runner (see Fig. 89). Before or during a service reception player I must have reached his setting position at the net between position II and III. The first pass comes high and diagonally so that with a parallel set the runner can use the forward-court players as attackers. Afterwards

Fig. 89

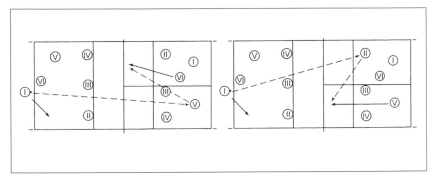

Fig. 93 a / b

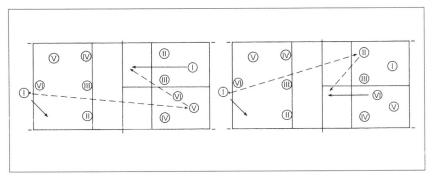

Fig. 94 a / b

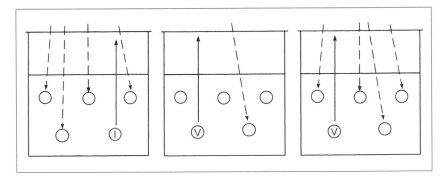

Fig 95 a / b

Game Form 3.2

Game structure: 5:5
Court size: 9 x 6m, later 9 x 9m
Rules:
Play in accordance with the game rules, but an additional point is given for each successful attack after setting with free runner (I or V) (see Fig. 91 a/b).

Variations on Game Form 3.2

1. Game structure: 5:5
Rules:
As above, but backcourt player I should always act as runner, except if he has to receive. In this case runner V will take over setting (Fig. 95 a/b).

2. Game structure: 5:5
Rules:
As above, but backcourt player V should act as runner; if he has to receive, position I will run (Fig. 95 c).

Coaching Points:
- As a backcourt player, anticipate early whether running is to be done by you.
- If the first pass is high and accurate, vary the attackers for spiking.
- Avoid errors if the first pass is inaccurate or travelling fast, and use a high pass to involve the attacker who is the easiest for you to set to.
- As a runner, leave the forward zone as soon as possible if the first pass is so inaccurate that you cannot do the setting.
- Decide early about the progression of the attack with running or second pass from the backcourt.
- Be ready as a backcourt player, but also as a frontcourt player, to do the setting if the first pass is inaccurate.
- When receiving, the player who moves forward to the setting area (calling out) has priority.

Game Form 3.3

Game structure: 6:6
Court size: 9 x 9m
Rules:
As for Game Form 3.3 above, the line-up and attack are the same as game 6:6 (see variation (2) of the game form).

3. Game structure: 6:6
Rules:
Offence from the 6-player pattern via frontcourt (1) or backcourt players (2) (see Fig. 108).

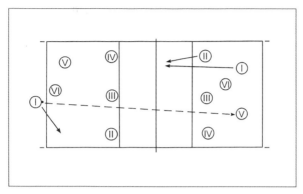

Fig. 108

Observation Points:
* Is it understood that the jump set can be executed more accurately than the drive?
* Is the drive still considered as a suitable action to hit to the opponent's court?

Learning Check-list
1. Can each player use a jump set to play a ball (thrown up by themselves) over the net to targets (mat of 2 x 2m) on the attack line and on the base line five times in a row without errors (see Fig. 109).
2. Can each player execute the jump set five times in a row against the wall or the basketball board without errors?

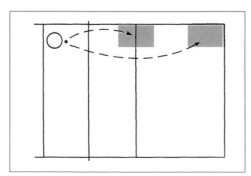

Fig. 109

Errors/Corrections to Jump Set

! **Errors in timing**
- Errors and drills are described in Lesson 1 (Roll shot/Drive) of LO 3 and in Lesson 2 (Attack) of LO 5.

! **Errors in the Contact Point and Body-ball-relationship**
- Errors and drills are described in Session 1 (front volley pass) of LO 1.

! **Errors in Giving Impetus**
- Missing arm-bending/extension prior to setting instead of pronounced arm-bending and fast extension.

Suggested Solutions:
1. Throws with heavy balls while sitting, from a setting position to high targets.
2. From a sitting position hit balls thrown by yourself or accurately by someone else to high targets, afterwards over a line/net to targets.

Session 2: Frontal Attack

Fig. 110

Action Sequence (Fig. 110)

The movement sequence of the front attack is to a great extent identical with that of the drive. The biggest difference is in the body-ball-relationship and the point of contact of the ball. In the case of a drive the **take-off point of the jump** is under the ball, while in the case of an offensive shot it is behind the ball.

As for the **body-ball-relationship**, with a drive the player is below the ball at the moment of ball contact, but with an attack shot he is behind and under the ball. In this way it is possible to ensure that with an attack shot the ball is hit from behind and above and deliberately and with powerful **wrist bend**, straight downwards. As all the other movements of the attack shot are fully identical with the drive, the further details are not dealt with in this chapter, and reference is made to LO 3 (see page 77).

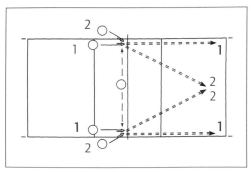

We talk about a frontal attack if the spike/smash hits the ball in an extension of his spike/smash approach direction. Depending on the direction the attacker can hit **down the line** (1) or **across court** (2) (see Fig. 111).

Fig. 111

Explanation

The attacker approaches according to the set, jumps and hits the ball with one hand straight downwards into the opponent's court to get the right to serve and to score a point (see Fig. 112).

Fig. 112

Game Form 2.1

Game structure: Spike/smash to targets
Court size: 9 x 9m – diagonal court.
Objective:
Players should master the attack shot as the most effective targeted move and use it accurately as a down the line or diagonal spike/smash. The player should realize that the smash should be accurate either down line and/or crosscourt.

Rules:
1. Groups of four (five or six) play against each other.
2. One of the players stands in between position IV and III and feeds the ball carefully with both hands, to a height about 3m above the top of the net.

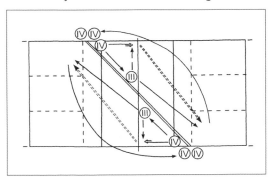

Fig. 113

3. The other players are in position IV in a line, whereby the first player spike/smash the thrown ball over the net to a target (goal/mat) in position V.
4. There is then a change of role. The spiker feeds, the feeder collects the ball and goes to the end of the attackers line (see Fig. 113).

Landing is done elastically on both feet on the take-off spot and should allow immediate game readiness. With regard to the timing of the blocker, the following applies: the blocking player takes off later than the spike/smash.

The ability to do this is based on the following factors:

- Assuming the same athletic capabilities, the spiker/smasher will jump higher than the blocker, because he jumps after an approach.
- According to the game rules, the smasher is not allowed to touch the ball over the net simultaneously with the blocker, but only after him, so the ball will travel from the spiker/smasher to the blocker.

The greater the difference is, between the jumping height of the spiker/smasher and the blocker, and the further the ball travels from the net (long ball trajectory), the more necessary it is to have time compensation by using a later take-off. Also, other different types of techniques, such as windmill spike/smash, faked attacks (dump/tip shots) and turning shots, can also lead to a later take-off.

Explanation

The blocker moves taking note of the set and the approach angle of the smasher to the take-off spot, jumps from both feet shortly after sender tries to defend the shot with both hands over the net and return the ball to the opponent's court (Fig. 125).

Game Form 1.1

Game structure: 1:1
Court size: 1.5 x 3m
Objective:
The player should experience the single block as an effective defence and offence element against the attack shot, and apply it as a passive or active block as the situation required.
The rules:
1. The players stand on both sides of the net
2. The ball is brought into play by a throw above the net.
3. Both players use active blocking if possible to try to push the ball into the opponent's court (one point).
4. Each player gets to throw the ball ten times (see Fig. 125); the winner is the player with the most points.
5. Touching the net and crossing with the feet over are errors and result in a point for the opponent

Fig. 125

Coaching Points

- In order to block, the blocking player jumps directly after the spike/smash.
- As a blocker take your ready position close to the net.
- As a blocking player keep your eye on the ball trajectory and time your take off so that the ball is contacted at the peak of the jump.
- Avoid touching the net by arching your hips during blocking and by moving your arms back behind/up before landing.
- Hold your hands with fingers spread about half a ball apart in order to cover a bigger area.
- Block passively when there is insufficient jumping height/reach and hold your hands in extension of the top of the net.
- Block actively when there is sufficient jumping/reach height by reaching across to the opponent's court with outstretched arms and hit the ball downwards to the floor with active wrist bending.
- Jump from and land on both feet.

Observation Points

- Is it necessary to refer to EE? because the execution of blocking causes great difficulties or there is insufficient athletic ability?
- Is the reason for touching the net not using the bending position, or incorrect arm movement?

Coaching Points:
- Is active blocking applied more often?
- Must the attack shot be further improved in order to make situation-specific blocking possible?
- Does the blocking player still keep an eye on the ball after his movement, and is he immediately ready to play again?

Variations on Game Form 1.2

1. After the successful block the attacking team can again attack if the rebound can be played again, just as the defensive team can attack after successful defence. Each error gives a point to the other team.
2. Same as Game Form 2 and variation 1 above, but the ball gets into play by serving and is received in three player pattern (see Fig. 129).
3. Game 3:3 according to the full rules of the game.

Court size: 3 x 6m, later 3 x 9m and 4.5 x 9m

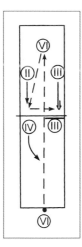

Special Rule:
For each successful single block the team wins one additional point.

Fig. 129

Observation Points:
- Has the introduction of the single block contributed to an improvement in the defence?
- Has the introduction of the smash and block increased motivation?

Coaching Point:
Block or move from the net.

Learning Check-List:
- Can each player successfully block the smash at least six times out of ten?
- The attacker stands higher on a box in position IV and smashes the ball thrown by her/himself to a prescribed target (2 x 2m) in position I (see Fig. 130).

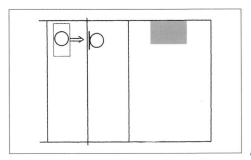

Fig. 130

Errors/Corrections to the Single Block

! Errors in the 'Ready' Position and Take-off

The player stands waiting for the opponent's attack at a distance instead of close to the net.
- The player's 'ready' position on the take-off spot is too upright instead of a medium-high or low position.
- The player hops prior to take-off or jumps from one foot instead of from both feet.

Suggested Solutions:
- The partners face each other at the net:
  a) Jump and touch each other with the palms of their hands across the net.
  b) The partners jump and pass the ball to each other across the net.
- Stationary balls, i.e. balls held over the top of the net are blocked from a distance of 1m, one after the other.
- Partner 'A' moves with the ball in a small area parallel and close to the net, partner 'B' tries to follow quickly. 'A' jumps whenever he wants and holds the ball over the top of the net. Later 'A' throws the ball with both hands over the net downwards to the forward court 'B' blocks actively or passively.

! Errors in Timing

Too early or too late take-off, i.e. prior to, or with the attacker, instead of directly after the attacker due to:

Observations Point:
- Is it necessary to refer to EE as there are problems with the actions at the net, especially in coverage?

Variations on Game Form 2.1

1. **Game structure:** 3:3, but with 3 frontcourt players (Figs. 135 and 131/132).
   Court size: 6 x 4.5m
2. **Game structure:** 4:4 (Fig. 136)
   Court size: 6 x 6m
3. **Game structure:** 2:2 (Fig. 137)
   Court size: 4.5 x 4.5m

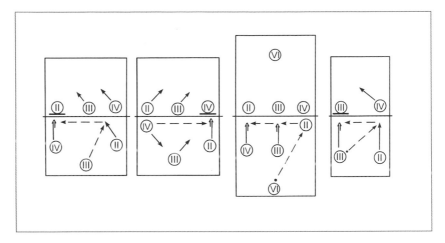

Fig. 135 a/b   *Fig. 136*   *Fig. 137*

4. Game form and variations, but the ball is put into play with a serve, and is received in three, four, or two man passing units.

Coaching Points:
- As a net player stand close to the net and be ready to block when your team serves or the opponent plays the ball.
- As a net player stand behind the attack line in the pattern in a service reception pattern when the opponent is serving.
- Move from the net to behind the attack line when the ball is on your own court.

Observation Points:
*   Does the setter also move to cover the attack?
*   Do the frontcourt players change their positions at the net in time according to the game situation offence or defence.

Game Form 2.2

Game structure: 3:3
Court size: 4.5 x 6m, later 4.5 x 9m with two frontcourt and one backcourt player
Rules:
Play according to the rules of the game, but with special rule: one additional point after each successful attack from coverage (Fig. 134).

Variations on Game Form 2.2

1. Game structure: 4:4
Court size: 6 x 6m, later 9 x 6m with three frontcourt and one backcourt players (Fig. 138).

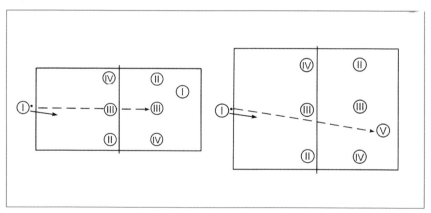

Fig. 138

2. Game structure: 6:6
Court size: 9 x 9m
Rules:
1. Reception in 6-player pattern.
2. Attack first via frontcourt players, later via backcourt players.
3. Team lines-up at own and opponent's serve and at attack and defence with single block as shown in Fig. 139 a-d.

The introduction of the 5-player pattern with the setter in position III is the lead in **position-specific attack formation** (see "Learning Objectives", page 16). The position-specific attack formation enlarges the offence possibilities as it gives the receiver alternative options for actions and decisions. This means there is a change in the significance of the possible decisions, priority should be given to making the first pass to position III. Should this create the risk of inaccuracy and/or result in subsequent errors, the receiver should revert to the use of the systematic offence second pass from the backcourt by executing a safe high pass to the middle of the court. The position-specific attack requires greater skills by the receiver with regard to the accuracy of the first pass. The receiver has to pass the ball to a given position at the net from any part of the court. In order to facilitate reception and to minimize errors in service, the serve should always be executed from the middle service area.

The attack via frontcourt player in position III is introduced based on the following considerations:
The setter in position III:
- Is centrally placed and at approximate equal distance to all receiving team-mates.
- Only requires the receivers to make a slight body turn.
- Only has to make short or medium distance passes.
- Only has to run short distances and make slight body turns before setting (except for reception in position VI).
- Can more easily compensate for inaccurate first passes thanks to the central position.

Session 1: Tip/Dump

Action Sequence

The movement sequence of T/D attacking tipping is the same as spiking/ smashing, except for the **ball contact phase** (see LO 5). The player approaches as in smashing/spiking, jumps using both legs and draws back ready to strike, but just before contact, the player stops the hitting action and executes a volley pass with one or both hands. In order to get the ball upward over the block. He pitches the ball from below and behind using all fingers, or to get the ball down past the block, from above and behind. When passing the ball over the block **impetus** comes from extending the still slightly bent hitting arm, – or again after a striking movement. The final impetus, especially to a ball played downwards, is given by **bending of the wrist** (see Fig. 141). The landing is on two feet, i.e. the same as in the case of a spike/smash.

Fig. 141   Fig. 142

Explanation

The attacker jumps and extends to execute an attack shot and pretends to spike/smash but stops the movement before contacting the ball, and passes the ball either with one or two hands over the block, or next to the block, to a gap in the frontcourt (Fig. 142).

Game Form 1.1

Game structure: Individual Competition
Court size: 4.5 x 3m
Objective:
The players should get to know the T/D as an attacking technique and experience the use of this further technique as an alternate of offence and to feint the opponent. The player should further be able to use it depending on the block situation and his own abilities.
Rules:

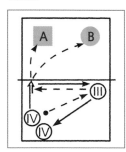

1. The player in position IV does a dump/tip attack after throwing/setting from position III over the net to a target (A) on the forward court.
2. Afterwards the attacker becomes setter and vice versa (Fig. 143).
3. The winner is the player to get the most targets out of 10/20.

Fig. 143

Coaching Points:
- Before execution of a dump/tip always feint the extension of the arm and the hitting movement for a spike/smash.
- The surprise moment increases, as later, you can release a tip/dump.
- Stop your hitting movement just short before you touch the ball.
- Set the ball with one arm and with low arm extension and little use of the wrist.
- Set the ball with flexible fingers.
- Dump/tip the ball from under and behind to play the ball over the block; dump/tip the ball from above and behind to play it beside the block to the floor.
- Play the attack on an uncovered area in the middle and backcourt defence area with both hands. Use one hand when you play into the frontcourt.
- Be careful that the motion for attack is the same as for a spike/smash; the touch phase is similar to the setting.
- Use the attack if the block is placed very well and a spike/smash to pass the block is very difficult to execute.

Observation Points:
- Is it necessary to refer to EE because there are weaknesses in the impetus/ touch point or the T/D attack isn't executed as a similar movement to the spike/smash?
- Is already the use of the one-handed set as a feint spike/smash a difficulty, so that it is better to use both arms?

Variations on Game Form 1.1

Court size: 6 x 3m
1. T/D attack on target (B) (Fig. 143), later to A and B alternately.
2. T/D attacking is executed in position II after throwing/setting from position III, first to target 'A', later to target 'B'.
3. T/D attacking is executed in position III after throwing/setting from position II, first to target 'A', later to target 'B' and 'C' (see Fig. 144). Court size: 6 x 3m.
4. The T/D attack is executed against a blocker standing on a box, later jumping to block. (The attacker becomes the setter. The setter becomes blocker, while the blocker becomes attacker (Fig. 145).

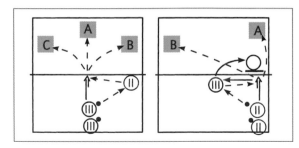

Fig. 144/145

Game Form 1.2

Game structure: 3:3
Court size: 4.5 x 4.5m
Rules:
1. Three ball contacts are compulsory, the third is a T/D attack against a single block (see Fig. 146).
2. At breaks in play both groups, each consisting of two frontcourt and one backcourt players, rotate.
3. The winner is the group of 6 players with the longest rally.

Variations on Game Form 1.2

1. **Game structure:** 3:3
   Court size: 6 x 3m (three frontcourt players – Fig. 147).
2. **Game structure:** 4:4
   Court size: 6 x 4.5m, later 9 x 4.5m (three frontcourt players/one backcourt player – Fig. 148).
3. **Game structure:** 2:2
   Court size: 4.5 x 3m (two forward-court players – see Fig. 142).

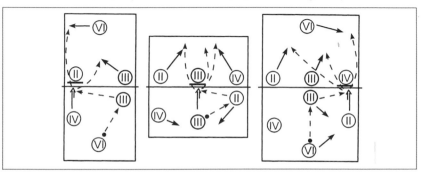

Fig. 146   Fig. 147   Fig. 148

Game Form 1.3

Game structure: Against each other
Rules:
1. The games with each other (see Game Form 1.2 and variations) are played according to the rules of the game.
2. The offence can be either executed situation- or position-specific.
3. Special rule: one additional point is awarded for a successful T/D attack, with two additional points for a successful single block.

Variations on Game Form 1.3

1. Game structure: 3:3, later 4:4
Court size: 4.5 x 9m
Special rule: One additional point for each successful offensive/blocking action.

2. Game structure: 4:4
Court size: 6 x 9m

3. Game structure: 6:6
Court size: 9 x 9m

Observation Points:
• Does the T/D attack cause major problems for the opposing team and does this lead to frequent breaks in play?
• Has the introduction of the attack resulted in T/D attacking being used more often than the spike/smash?
• Does dump/tip attacking help make offence more varied and dynamic?
• Are spike/smash, T/D attacks and roll shots used according to the situation?

Learning Check-List:
• Can each player execute a dump/tip attack at least five times out of ten over the block or past the block to different targets on the frontcourt?
• The attacker in position IV gets the pass thrown from position III and executes a T/D attack alternately to target 'A' and 'B' (1 x1 m) over the standing block (players on box/block, see Fig. 149).

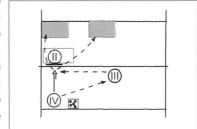

Fig. 149

Errors/Corrections of T/D Attack

! Errors in Movement

The player:

- Does not run nor take an approach.
- Do not swing both arms.
- Does not draw back before hitting and lets his intentions be recognized too early by raising his arms directly to the ball (no feigning of the hit).
- Times the jumping action badly.

Suggested Solutions:

All the drills for the errors of front spike/smashes (LO 5/Session 2) making sure of ball contact in one-handed volley after feigning the hanging action.

! Errors in Impetus and in the Contact Point

- The ball is played with the palm or not with all fingers of the hitting hand (e.g. without thumbs).
- The player does not stop the movement suddenly, but plays the ball with extended arm and throws the ball (rule contravention).
- Ball contact takes too long and the player extends the arm too late so the ball is carried (rule contravention).
- The arm is slightly bent and extended at instead of prior to the ball contact (ball held or carried).

Suggested Solutions:

- Volley passes with one hand quickly in succession, later alternating with the right and left hand (at the beginning with lighter balls).
- One-handed jump sets from a short distance against the wall (basketball board).
- Partner drills at the net, the ball is set with one hand while jumping (one with one).
- Drills where the ball is first thrown by the player himself, later thrown/set by the partner is played one-handed to the target placed high but close (e.g. basketball hoop), first in standing, later in jumping with feigned hitting movement.
- See also drills for rule contraventions in case of errors in volley (LO 1/Session 1) and in spiking (LO 5/Session 2).

Session 2: 5-player Pattern with Attack via Forward-court Player in Position III

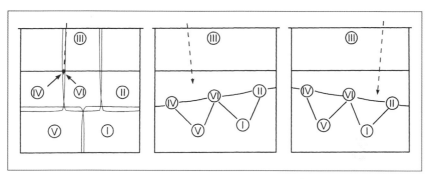

Fig. 150   Fig. 151 a   Fig. 151 b

Action Sequence (see Figs. 150-152)

In the 5-player pattern the **players in the front row (IV/VI/II)** cover the whole area of the front and middle-court. Standing about 1-2m behind the attack line, the distance of each to the server is about the same.

The **players in the back positions (I and V)** cover the backcourt and stand about 2-2.5m from the base line, opposite gaps in the front line.

Together with the frontcourt players and position VI they form two triangles of equal size ("W"-formation).

The exact defence area of the 5-player pattern is shown in Fig. 150.

In the case of position-specific offence the basic rule is, if the ball is travelling to **the edges of the areas of responsibility**, that the player who is moving in the direction to the setter should receive it. He should therefore be in a position to play as frontally as possible in the direction in which he is running.

The **setter** at the net should position her/himself (with his right shoulder to the net) so as to see both the server and the pattern of play. They should not block his team-mates' view of the server. Should the serve not be executed from the middle of the service area (position VI) but from the right corner (position I), the 5-player pattern is as shown in Figs. 151 a and 152. When the serve comes from the left side of the service area (i.e. position V), the pattern is positioned according to Fig.151 b.

Explanation

Five players stand in 5-player 'W-formation' to receive the serve (see Fig. 152). The sixth player is out of the pattern and is placed in the frontcourt zone in position III to act as setter. The reception and the pass of the serve is played position-specific, and goes to the setter in position III who sets the ball to the attacker in positions IV or II with a volley pass parallel to the net forwards or backwards.

Fig. 152

Game Form 2.1

Game structure: 2:6
Court size: 9 x 9m
Objective:
The players should experience and use the 5-player pattern with attack via position III as an adequate formation which offers suitable court coverage to receive serves, and allows easy position-specific transition to attack.

Rules:
1. The two players pass the serve alternately over the net.
2. The team on the opposite court takes the 5-player line-up and builds the attack on setter in position III.
3. One point is awarded for each action that successfully ends with a smash from position IV or II.
4. After four serves the eight players rotate one position (see Fig. 153).
5. The winner is the group with the most points after 32 serves.

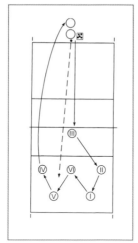

Fig. 153

Coaching Points:

- In case of easy serves play the first pass accurately to the setter in position III in the frontcourt, and in case of difficult serves, high to the middle of the court to initiate the attack with the second pass from the backcourt.
- Check your position in the pattern in relation to team-mates and to the sideline, base-line and attack line.
- Communicate clearly and early with your team-mates.
- The player who moves in the direction of the setter has priority in receiving the serve.
- As a receiver play in front of the body after moving and turning, and always play high and not too close to the net.

Observation Point:

- As there are errors in the line-up of the 5-player pattern, and/or the movement and targeting of the first pass is not accurate, and there are problems with the attack via position III, is it necessary to refer to EE?

Variations on Game Form 2.1

1. One additional point is awarded for each successful attack after a reverse set.

2. **Game structure:** As Game 2.1 above, but each target hit is followed by rotation and an additional exercise (e.g. jumping from a crouch – spike/ smash from approach, etc.).

3. **Game structure:** As individual competition:
   Each player gets five serves in succession. The server gets a point each time the opposing team cannot end the offence with a successful spike/smash. The winner is the player of the 8-player group who gets the most points.

4. **Game structure:** Group competition of three players in game 3:3:
   Rules:
   One member of the 3-man group (A) is the server, the two others form a single block in positions IV and II. The group of six takes the formation of the 5-player pattern with setter in position III and this group is in turn divided into two groups of three. Group 1 (B) consists of the forward-court players, Group 2 (C) of the backcourt players (see Fig. 154.).

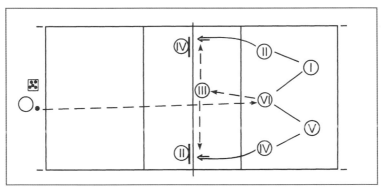

Fig. 154

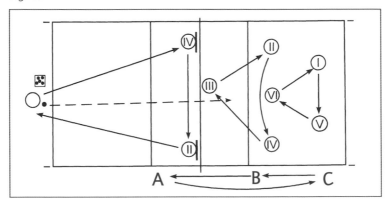

Fig. 155

Each player has five serves, whereby the groups of three rotate within the group after each series of serves. After 15 serves the groups change responsibilities: group A becomes C, C becomes B and B becomes A (see Fig. 155).

Each action of the 3-player group earns a point if it is finished with a successful attack shot. A point is given for each successful block to the attack shot if rebounded or blocked touches balls can be saved, a repeated attack is allowed. The winner is the group of three players with the most points.

Game Form 2.2

Game structure: 6:6
Court size: 9 x 9m
Rules:
1. Both teams line up both for the serve reception and for defence of the attack (defence without blocking) in 5-player pattern with setter in position III (see Fig. 156).

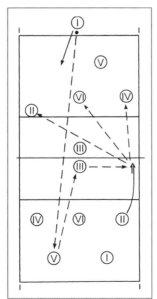

Fig. 156

2. Three ball contacts are compulsory; the third one is either a jump set or a roll shot. The winner is the group of twelve with the longest series of net crossings.

- Is it necessary to remind players of the attack with a second pass via back-court?
- Is it necessary to change the 5-player pattern? Is it necessary to have closer alignment (line pattern) because most serves are long (see Fig. 160 a), or should the pattern be more spread out as serves vary with regard to distance and direction (see Fig. 160 b)?

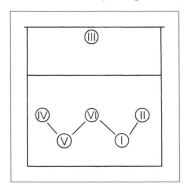

Fig. 160 a

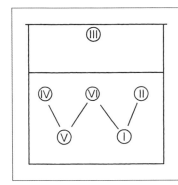

Fig. 160 b

- Must the receiving formation be changed because the server is serving either from the right or left side of the service area (see Fig. 151 a/b).

Learning Check-List:
1. Students can answer test questions (with the help of sketches) concerning:
   a) The receiving area and responsibilities of the players in the pattern.
   b) The prerequisites and movements of the position-specific attack with frontcourt player in position III.
   c) The possibilities of transition from receiving/defence to attack after inaccurate first passes.
2. Free observation of the 5-player pattern with attack via frontcourt player in position III taking into consideration above a)-c).

! **Errors/Corrections of 5-player Pattern**

Errors in the execution of the first pass as a result of insufficient accuracy of movements and targeting

Suggested Solutions:
- Repeat drills to improve digging (see LO/Session 2 and LO 4, Session 1).
- Triple pass exercises with/without run (see Figs. 161-164).

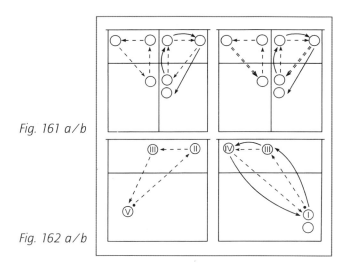

Fig. 161 a/b

Fig. 162 a/b

- Drills where balls are thrown/volleyed/hit over the net are received and accurately passed to position III (see Fig. 165).
- Drills where reception is linked with setting (from position III), and attack first with one, later with both attackers II + IV (see Figs. 166 and 167).

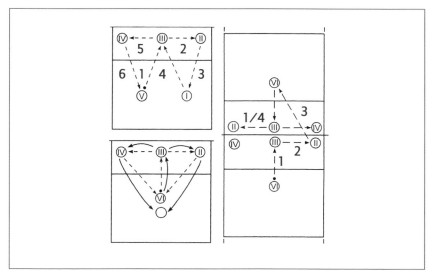

Figs. 163 a/b   *Fig. 164*

Learning Objective 8:

The Dig – Single Block and Backcourt Defence with Position VI Back

Fig. 168

Situational Analysis

Having learnt the single block, plus the introduction of the position-specific attack via the setter in position III, which should have improved the teams attacking potential. It is now necessary to create more balance in play and create an efficient transposition from defence to attack it will now be necessary to introduce the dig.

Tactics – When to Use the Dig

The Double-arm Dig

To cope with fast hard attacking shots, and be able to keep the ball in play the team need to be capable of digging the ball from all positions on the court.

When they are able to do this consistently, then they should be able to set up a counter-attack using the frontcourt players as setter, or if necessary by using a player from the back row to set the ball to create an attacking play.

To defend the opposition's attack, the team should adopt a **block and backcourt defence with the player in position VI having moved back** to deal with the deep hit.

When this happens it is essential that the other five players should cover the backcourt including covering the block and the defending court (see Fig. 168). This type of activity involves not only individual player's technical skills, but also collaboration and co-operation between the back defenders and blockers. To achieve this, the coach should work on the **single block** and **backcourt defence** with the player in position VI moved well back in the court.

The decision to adopt this strategy is based on the following considerations:

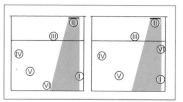

Fig. 169   Fig. 170

1. There is only a single blocker with an adjacent player covering.

2. The entire backcourt is covered by the backcourt players.

3. If the player in position VI has moved forward, thus creating an overlap with the backcourt defenders.

4. Only the introduction of the double block can justify the introduction of block and backcourt defence with the player in position VI moving forward (see LO 10).

Technique – How to Play the Dig

Fig. 173

Session 1 – The Dig

Fig. 171   Fig. 172

Action Sequence – The Dig (see Fig. 171)

The sequencing of movement for the dig is very similar to that used in the dig set (see LO 1 and 2). The difference lies in the involvement of the arms and legs, and the ready position in preparation to receive the ball. The faster and lower the flight of the ball, the lower the ready position and the less the arms and legs are involved. If the ball is travelling very hard and low, the receiver should merely attempt to absorb the force of the ball and "re-direct" it by relaxing the arms when making contact. If the ball is extremely low, then the player may need to roll in order to prevent it touching the ground and providing a means of absorbing the force of the ball (see LO 11, Session 1).

Like the dig set, the two-handed dig in a standing position can be carried out both to the front and the side (see Fig. 172 and LO 4/Session 1).

Explanation

The defender should be reading the game constantly, following not only the ball, but also the positions and actions of the opposition. Once he judges that it is necessary, they should adopt the ready position (Fig. 173). If the ball is travelling fast and hard he must defend it by using a two-handed dig either to the front, or side of the body. **N.B.** It is very important in this case not to involve too much leg action as this will only add to the terminal velocity of the ball, and make it harder to set up an efficient counter-attacking move by passing high to the setter or the middle of the court.

Game Forms

The following Game Forms will help you to emphasise the elements of skill on which you are working.

Game Form 1.1

Game structure: 2:1
Court size: 3 x 9 m
Objective:
The 2-man offensive team must put pressure on the single defending player who should learn to use a two-handed dig as the most efficient technique to keep fast moving balls in play.
Rules:
The defender earns a point if he can:

1. Save the ball, so it remains in the attacker's court.
2. Create a forced error on the part of the attacker.
3. After 10 attempts the players rotate positions.
4. The winner is the player who has scored the most points.

Variations on Game Form 1.1

The defender only earns a point if he can play the ball he saved.

Coaching Points:
- The lower the ball, the lower the ready position.
- The faster the ball, the more passive/relaxed the arms and legs.
- Keep eyes on the attacker to pick up early cues as to the direction and force the attack.
- Move as early as possible from the backcourt using small quick steps into the ready position, before the ball arrives. This should bring the defender under and behind the ball.
- The body weight should be evenly balanced on both feet with the centre of gravity moved over the balls of the feet.

Learning Check-List:
Are there still problems in players dealing with movement to the dig, and accuracy of passing? If yes, it I may be necessary to refer to the section EE. As a coach do you think that it is necessary/advisable to train speed of movement and reaction separately?

Game Form 1.2

Game structure: 1:1 with a shared setter
Court size: 3 x 9m
Objective:
Defence in game situation plus the link from defence to attack.
Rules:
1. The ball to be brought into play by an attacking hit after the first set (see Fig. 174 a), and then later brought into play by a serve (Fig. 174 b).
2. The setter always goes to the side of the team-mate handling the ball.
3. Everyone plays a set against each other, after which roles and responsibilities are changed.
4. Apart from this the normal rules of the game apply.

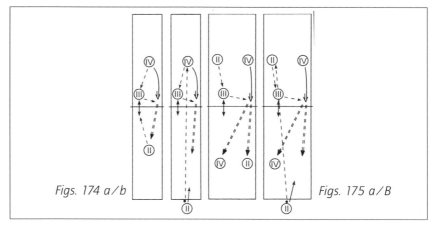

Figs. 174 a/b   Figs. 175 a/B

Game Form 1.3

Game structure: 2:2 with a shared setter (Fig. 175 a/b)
Court size: 4.5 x 9m
Objective:
Players are only allowed to dig to the side of the body if it is not possible to position the body under and behind the ball.

Rules:
1. After setting, one of the two teams must play a smash after setting, while the other defends.
2. The defenders get a point if the ball can be caught by one of their team.
3. After 10 smashes the players change places with a partner.

N.B. The coach should be evaluating the strength of the defenders by observing the quality of play that follows a defensive dig.

Game Form 1.4

Game structure: 2:2
Court size: 3 x 9m, later 4.5 x 9m
Objective:
One team executes an attack after setting, the other team defends.
Rules:
1. The defenders score a point if either of them can catch the ball following a dig.

2. Only the actual digger may catch the ball and score the point.
3. After 10 attacks the players change positions.
4. After 20 attacks the attacking and defending teams change over.

Variations on Game Form 1. 4

1. The defenders score a point if they can pass the ball over the net following a dig and if they can carry out an effective counter-attack.
2. Play a 3:3 game (Fig. 177) on a court sized 4.5 x 9m using variation 1 as the basic rules.

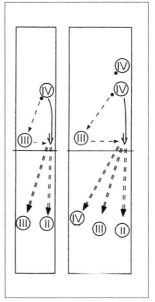

Figs. 176 and 177

Learning Check-List:
- Does the ball hit the ceiling, or is it played back directly to the opposition? If yes, then it has been hit too hard, i.e. with too much impetus.
- Are there frequent breaks in the flow of play after the court defence? If yes, then the ball has been played too low following a defensive dig because the ready position was too high; or the ball has been hit out of court because the defender moved too late; or to the incorrect position to receive the ball.
- Are there frequent breaks in play?
- If yes, it is probably because players are using their feet as a means of defending?
- Are players aware that balls arriving at shoulder level can be played with a single volley as opposed to a dig set?
- If yes, this is because double contact in defence play is not penalised.
- Do players select appropriate shots to play a dig or a dig set?
- Do court defenders cover each other at difficult times?

- Player A feeds the ball hard and accurately.
- Player A feeds the ball hard and inaccurately.
- Player A hits the ball from the frontcourt to player B in the backcourt, who digs the ball back or high to the centre of the court (see Fig. 181 a/b).

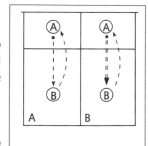

Fig. 181 a/b

2. Triangle work:

- Players A and B hit the ball alternatively to player C who returns a dig to either feeder, or to the centre of the court (see Fig. 182).
- Player A volleys the ball to player B who in turn hits it to C, who defends A who volleys again to B and so on (see Fig. 183).
- Player A hits to C, who digs to B. B hits to C who digs to A (see Fig. 184).

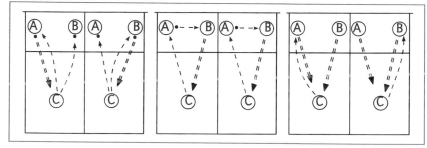

Fig. 182   *Fig. 183*   *Fig. 184*

3. Additional partner work:

- Player A volleys to B, who hits to A who digs to B who volleys to A and so on.
- Player A stands on a box and throws or hits the ball over the net to player B who digs either into the frontcourt or the centre of the court (see Fig. 185 a).
- As above, but the ball is smashed after setting and is saved by digging (see Fig. 185b).

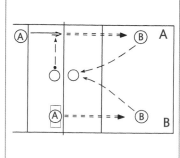

Figs. 185 a/b

Session 2: Single Block with Backcourt Defence with Position VI Back

Situational Analysis – Defending an Attacking Move

When anticipating an attacking move the defending team should adopt a backcourt alignment outside and to the rear of the base-line (see Fig. 186) with the player at position VI lying deep, and with the frontcourt players standing close to the net (0.5m).

When playing a single block, the remaining player(s) next to the blocker cover/s the block, with the remaining players forming a semi-circle. It is possible to form a single block at all three net positions (see Figs. 168/169/187/188). When using this formation the blocking player must try to cover the main direction of the attacker. The use of this formation, known as the **'block shadow'**, allows the defenders to see those areas of the backcourt that are not covered. In order to be able to see both the ball and the attacker the other defenders must position themselves outside the block screen. It is very important that all the defending players have anticipated the attacker's move and are in place prior to the attack taking place. If they are to be successful, the defenders (except position VI) should only have to move forwards and sideways and not backwards. In other words they have **2/3rds of the court in front of them and only 1/3rd to the rear** (see Fig. 189). The benefits of this form of defence should be reflected in succeeding phase of the game, viz. setting and attack.

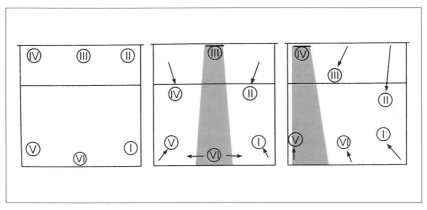

Fig. 186   Fig. 187   Fig. 188

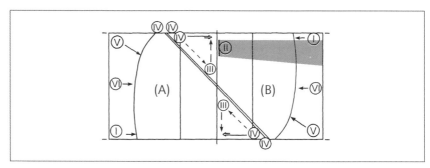

Figs. 192 a / b

Variations on Game Form 2.1

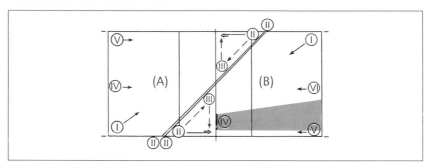

Figs. 193 a / b

1. The attacker starts from position II (see Fig. 193 a).
2. The attacker runs from position II (see Fig. 193 b).

Coaching Points:
- Players must always be prepared to cover a team-mate in a difficult defensive situation by moving closer to him.
- In critical situations players must communicate their intentions by calling out.

Game Form 2.2

Game structure: Defence 4:4
Court size: 4.5 x 9m
Rules:
1. The 4th player acts as a blocker or an attacker depending on the circumstances (see Fig. 192 b). It is possible to add an additional variation where the attacker runs from position II (see Fig. 193 b).

Coaching Points:
- The players should block the main direction of hitting.
- Players should play the role of defender to the block screen and defending outside it.

Game Form 2.3

Game structure: Defence 5:5
Court size: 9 x 9m
Rules:

1. The team plays without a player at position III and defends the opponents attacking from either position IV or II (see Figs. 194 a/b).
2. The defending team scores an additional point if the players can successfully return the ball over the net after 3 contacts, and an additional 2 points if the play ends in an attacking move.

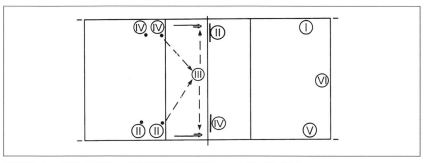

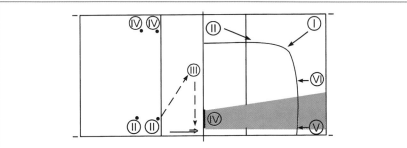

Figs. 194 a/b

Coaching Point:
- If there are problems with defensive alignments and teamwork in this game, you may need to refer to section EE.

For example:

TEAM	
A	B
25 – 20 – 5 points	19 – 25 + 6 points

6. To receive the serve the team may use either a 5- or 6-player pattern.

Learning Check-List:
- Does the defence go to the setter at the net or to the centre of the court (Target 3) or is it incorrect because of wrong positioning?

- Do you use all three ball contacts to get from defence to attack with a spike/smash?

- Do the defenders adopt positions that are appropriate to the block to deal with the attacking play? For example, the jump height or approach angle of the attacker or the distance of the setter from the net?

- Can students answer the following test questions, if necessary using sketches for guidance:
  1. What are the different alignments for backcourt defenders with a single block in positions II, III and IV?
  2. What is the significance of the block screen?
  3. What are the defensive responsibilities of players in different court positions?
  4. What are the tactical possibilities for transposition from defence to attack?

Observe the teams playing freely, i.e. without any conditions imposed. Watch the blocking and backcourt defence with position VI moved well back and taking into account points 1-4 above.

Errors and Corrections for Blocking and Backcourt Play

! 1. Problems with the Execution of the First Dig Pass due to Errors in Directional Accuracy or Lack of Correct Movement

Suggested Solution:
See EE for Session 1.

! 2. Errors and Misunderstandings in the Teamwork of Backcourt Defenders

Suggested Solutions:
- Work on exercises for defending attacking moves using at least two defenders, with balls hand-fed in between the players (see Fig. 198).
- See EE for Session 2 of LO 2 and 3, which deal with drills for creating teamwork between receivers/defenders.

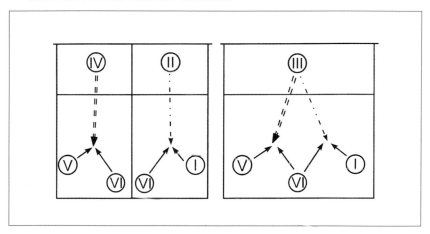

Figs. 198 a/b

! 3. Errors in Team Alignment with a Single Block in the Situation Where Position VI Has Moved Well Back
- The players are unaware of the defensive areas.
- The backcourt defenders are not evenly spaced out or in a semi-circle position.
- The backcourt defenders are not orientating themselves to the blocking screen and are standing in the screen itself.
- The frontcourt players are playing no part in defence and are not moving sufficiently early or far back enough.

Suggested Solutions:
- Revisit theoretical discussions regarding blocking and backcourt defending with a one-man block in different net positions.
- Include the possibilities of movement from defence to attack with the help of different coaching aids such as video or magna board.

- Renew discussions regarding the roles and responsibilities of different players within the given defensive formation.
- Repeat exercises using different methods, for example with a blocker on a box to raise his height. Hit attacking shots initially at an individual defender, then randomise them and change the target defenders (see Figs. 199a/b).

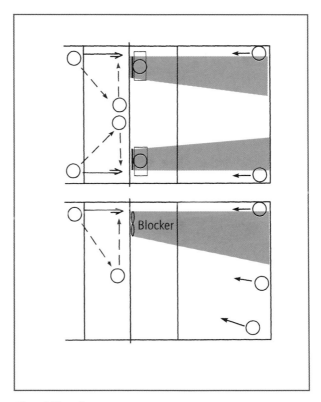

Figs. 199 a/b

LEARNING OBJECTIVE 9:

Short and Long Sets; 5-player Pattern with Attack via Setter in Position II

Fig. 200

Situational Analysis

The **5-player pattern with attack via frontcourt player II** (see contents of Session 2) represents the **extension of the position-specific offence action.** Here the frontcourt player in position II is not engaged in reception but acts as setter in the forward zone (see Fig. 200). Attack position III and position II make and give longer rallies both in receiving and passing and in setting the ball. The attack from position II using the 5-player pattern demands a higher level of technical and tactical skills by the players. It is important that players can use the targeted long cross-court and parallel passes as a prerequisite for rational use of this attack formation. These preconditions are dealt with in Session 1.

Given the above preconditions, a team using an attack progression with position II has the following advantages:

- The setter has a good view of the server, receiver and attacker and can therefore act sensibly with regard to individual tactics.
- Both attackers can be played to with a forward set, and right-handers have an advantage because of their hitting side.
- Observation of the opponent's responses, especially the blocking player, is easy for the setter. Consequently, attack combinations can be varied and formed to the advantage of the attacking team.

Fig. 211

Game Form 2.1

Game structure: 3:3 (Fig. 212)
Court size: 6 x 4m
Objective:
The players should experience and use the 5-player pattern with setter in position II as an addition to the position-specific attack with frontcourt player in which the setter can use both attackers with forward sets. They should be put in a position to use this situation specifically for an attack shot taking under consideration the quality of the first pass and the responses of the attackers.
Rules:
1. Three ball contacts are compulsory, where the third ball contact is either a jump set or a dump/tip attack.
2. The ball is put into play with a volley pass; and after a break in play the groups rotate.
3. The winners are the group of six with the longest series of net crossings.

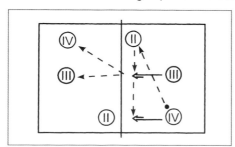

Fig. 212

Coaching Points:
Players should play:
- So that it is clear which of the two attackers will be used.
- Set the ball high or medium high to the attacker in position III over a medium distance.
- Set the ball high to the attacker in position IV over a long distance.
- As a setter use more bending and stretching for long passes.
- As receiver play the dig set over a long distance as forward as possible, with marked bending of the legs.

Observation Point:
- Is it necessary to refer to EE as the first pass does not come to the setter accurately. There are problems with high and long sets to the attacker?

Variations on Game Form 2.1

1. **Game structure:** 4:4 (see Fig. 213)
   Court size: 6 x 6m
2. As Game Form 2.1 above and variation (1) with the special rule that the players rotate one position after each ball pass over the net.

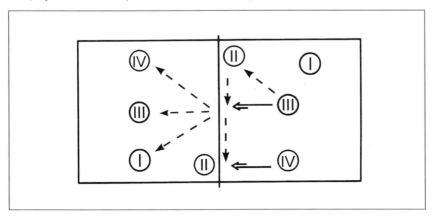

Fig. 213

Game Form 2.2

Targeted Spike/Smash from Position IV after Set from Position II (Fig. 214 a)
1. Execution same as Game Form 2.1 above and Game Form 2.3 of Session 2/ LO 4 .

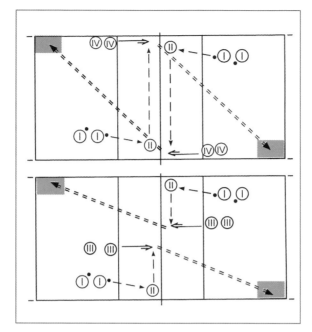

Figs. 214 a/b

2. Targeted spike/smash from position III after set from position II (see Fig. 214b).
   Court size: 4.5 x 9m

Game Form 2.3

Game structure: 4:4 (Fig. 215 a), later in 3:3 (Fig. 215 b)
Execution same as Game Form 1.1 above, and Game Form 2.4 and 2.5 of Session
2/LO 4.

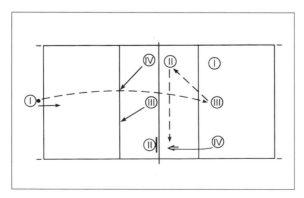

Fig. 215 a

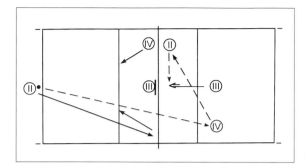

Fig. 215 b

Coaching Points:
- Play long passes frontally after completing turning of the body from a low bending position.
- When there is a high volley pass over a long distance, as attacker only start running when the ball has reached the peak of its trajectory.

Observation Points:
- Is the backcourt player in position II aware that he must move up to the first reception line of the pattern because frontcourt player II as been moved forward as setter?
- Has the co-ordination of the setter with the two attackers improved because he can observe the responses of both of them and set to both with forward sets?
- Is it necessary to train separately the teamwork of setters and attackers because either attacker IV or III is setting too much to one side?

Game Form 2.4

Game structure: 2:6 (see Figs. 216 a/b)
The execution is the same as in Game Form 2.2 and variations (1) to (4) of Game Form 2.1, Session 2/LO 7.
N.B. Regarding variation (1): the additional point is given for a successful attack shot from position IV after set from position II.

Coaching Points:
- Play the first pass high and not too close to the net to position II.
- Play the first pass more in front of than behind the setter.
- In the case of inaccurate first passes, volley the ball high and not too close to the net.
- As setter make yourself heard.

LEARNING OBJECTIVE 10:

Double Block – Block and Backcourt Defence with Position IV Moved Forward

Fig. 224

Situational Analysis

Based on the single block already covered in LO 6, the double block is introduced in Session 1, in which the focus is on the co-operation of blocking players among themselves. With the introduction of further attacking variations, and position-specific attacks via forward players (see LO 7 and 9) the basic situation set-attack is expected to be reinforced. Therefore the improvement of the basic situation is aimed for. It can be achieved by introducing the double block.

Compared to the single block the **double block** is a far more effective defensive element against hard hits; and it leaves smaller defence areas for backcourt defenders as the block screen area is bigger which helps improve defence overall. For the above reasons it is clear that the double block forces the attacker to vary the attack, whereby dump/tip attacking in particular is an adequate alternative. In order to counteract this, and to be able to cover the particularly endangered forward area of the block screen, the backcourt player in position IV is moved forward to **cover the double block**. Therefore this formation is called "block and backcourt defence with position IV moved forward". Position IV is best from which to cover the double block because the double block means the middle area of the backcourt is well-covered, assuming the block is well-positioned and close together.

Reasons for introducing the double block and backcourt defence with position IV moved forward or up:

- Each player has just one responsibility in defence, either as blocking, covering or defending a specific player.
- The defence areas, and also the responsibilities of the different players, are clearly determined and distinguished from each other.
- The defending players can basically perform their responsibilities without any additional athletic, tactical or technical prerequisites (e.g. diving dig set).
- The distribution of the defending players in three defence lines (block/ coverage/backcourt defence) guarantees even covering of the court (see Fig. 224).

Attacking with second pass from the backcourt is easier to execute because the backcourt player, moved forward in position IV, can take over setting because of his area of activity in the front part of the backcourt. Therefore, misunderstandings amongst players can to a large extent be avoided.

When learning blocking and backcourt defence it should be repeated at this point that the transposition from defence to attack must never be forgotten. The learning of defence is at the same time also learning to attack, as each defence action is followed by an attack.

Game Form 1.1

Game structure: 2:2
Court size: 3 x 6m
Objective:
The players should experience and use the double block as a very effective group-tactical defence action with offensive type characteristics. Depending on the players' abilities they should be able to form a double block actively or passively at all net positions, on the one hand to cover a large part of the court, and on the other to return the ball directly to the opponent's court.

Rules:
- The ball is put into play against a double block with an attacking shot instead of a set. Each group of two has twenty block and twenty attack attempts.
- After ten actions the players change their positions within the group, after twenty actions the groups change functions.
- The attacking group gets a point for each successful attack shot and for errors by the blocking players. The defending group gains a point for each successful double blocking and for errors by the attackers.
- The winners are the group with the most points in one or two sets.

Coaching Points:
- As an outside blocker, organize the double block and position yourself mainly to the ball and the attacker.
- As an inside blocker, assist the block and position yourself mainly to the ball and the outside blocker.
- Expect the opponent's attack close to the net with hands held in front of the chest.
- Move close along the whole net width to the block.
- Jump up vertically, both from standing and also after travelling across land at the take-off place if possible.
- While jumping and landing avoid touching your team-mates.
- While airborne, avoid any obstruction of the blocking team-mate or any contact with the net by raising your arms close to your body.
- As an outside block player, block the ball, as inside blocker block the area.
- When blocking, form as closed a defence area as possible with your team-mate.

Variations on Game Form 1.1

1. **Game as above,** but played as individual competition.
After twenty attacks the players change their responsibilities in predetermined order.

2. The blocking players must stand at least 2m apart prior to set.
3. As above, but on a court size 4.5 x 6m, with players standing 3-4m apart.

4. Game structure: 3:3
Court size: 6m x 6m. The set first comes from position III alternately to attackers IV and II, later at random to attacker IV or II (see Fig. 228).
5. Players to the attackers from positions II, III and IV (see Fig. 229).

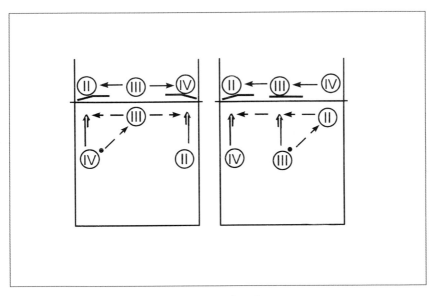

Fig. 228   Fig. 229

Observation Point:
• Because of risks of injuries from balls rolling uncontrolled at the net area is it necessary to remind players of safety measures (see page 28).

Coaching Points for Blocking Players:
• Watch the position of the setter to the ball in order to sense early the direction of the set.
• After moving to the block, take a strong stopping stride prior to take-off.
• The more frontal the approach to the take-off place is, the more the body must be turned in jumping.
• As a block-free player, move away from the net towards the attack line.

Learning Check-List:
- Can the players successfully defend the attack with a double block at least six times out of ten?
- The attacker stands raised on a box in position IV and spike/smashes the ball thrown up by him, to a determined target (4 x 2m) to position IV (see Fig. 233).
- After five attempts the outside and inside blockers change their positions.

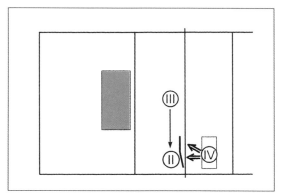

Fig. 233

Errors/Corrections of Double Block

All the exercises (LO 6/Session 1) in connection with the single block can be applied here as well.

! Errors in the Approach and Take-off Phase
- The approach is towards the net instead of close to and parallel with it.
- The penultimate step is too short to give the necessary impetus at take-off.
- As the player favours one leg, or jumps with little power, the point of take-off may not be the ideal, viz. identical with the landing place.

Suggested Solutions:
- Repeated discussion concerning ready position, approach and take-off possibilities of double block.
- Drills without the ball are practiced as a single block along the net/wall. Later handing the ball over while jumping, and finally blocking of the stationary/thrown ball.
- Drills with double block at all net positions, first without ball, later with standing/thrown/hit balls (see Fig. 234).
- In drills with stationary balls the court markings can serve as orientation.

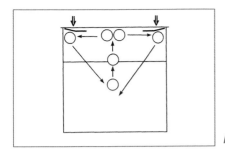

Fig. 234

! Errors in Arm Movement and Hand Position
- The players hold their hands wider or closer than half a ball-width apart.
- The outside blocker (IV and II) blocks the area instead of the ball.
- The inside blocker (III) blocks the ball instead of the area (diagonal).
- The blocking players make net errors because:
  - **a)** They swing their arms wide and high instead of bent and close to the body.
  - **b)** They do not assume a jackknife position in jumping, and they move their hands down instead of up and behind after blocking.

Suggested Solutions:
- Drills with attackers against a double block at low/diagonal net; attackers and blockers have no approach.
- Drills where the take-off place is determined:
  - **a)** The player stands on a box and after spiking/smashing towards the double block.
  - **b)** In jumping, the player spikes/smashes the ball fed to him towards the double block.
  - **c)** The player spikes/smashes the ball self fed towards the double block.

! Errors in Timing
- The blockers jump at the same time as the attacker instead of shortly after him.
- The assistant blocker approaches and jumps at the same time as the outside blocker, instead of prior to him.
- The outside blocking player only watches the ball trajectory instead of the ball and the attacker.
- The moving blocking player positions himself too much to the attacker instead of also taking the ball trajectory and team-mates into account.

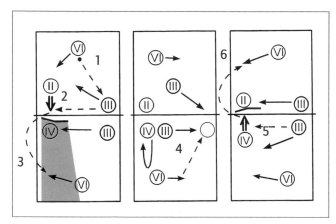

Figs. 245 a-c

Coaching Points:

- The backcourt player in position VI undertakes block coverage, while the backcourt players in positions I and V take over defence of the backcourt.
- As covering player in position VI, always move around the level of the attack line and the ball.
- As covering player VI, make sure that if there is a double block in position III you especially cover the area of the blocking player moving inside to the double block (position IV or II).

Variations on Game Form 2.1

1. Game structure: 4:4
Court size: 4.5 x 9m
Rules:
The third ball contact can be either a jump set or dump/tip attack or also a long drive. Two forward and two backcourt players make up the group whereby one is covering the block in position VI, and the other undertakes backcourt defence in position I or V (see Fig. 246).

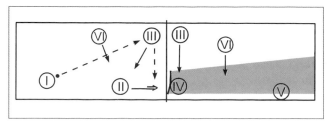

Fig. 246

Coaching Points:
- As a block covering player in position VI, take a low or medium-low ready position when the double block is formed.
- After the block, be ready to act as a setter and always watch the ball.
- As a block covering player play the first pass high, and not too close to the net, to the forward player.
- As a forward player, after executing the attack, immediately move to the net to prepare for blocking.

2. Game structure: 4:4
Court size: 6 x 4.5m, later 9 x 4.5m
Rules:
- Play is with three forward players and the backplayer in position VI as the block covering player.
- First the attack runs via position III (see Fig. 247), later via position II (see Fig. 248).

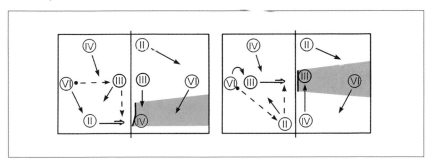

Figs. 247 & 248

Coaching Point:
- As a block-free forward-court player, move away from the net to the attack line in plenty of time before the execution of the attack shot.

Game Form 2.2

Game structure: 3:3
Court size: 4.5 x 4.5m
Rules:
An additional special rule, i.e. that the ball comes into play with attack after setting instead of serving (see Fig. 245).

Learning Objective 11:

Setting while Falling Backwards and Sideways – Attack Coverage 2:3 and 3:2 with Player in VI-Up Position

Fig. 253

Situational Analysis

The improvement of offence, in particular through the introduction of the double block, creates situations both for the attacking and the defending teams in which the ball may have a surprising and/or unpredictable change in direction. These are mostly deflections (off-the-block balls) which often fall quickly to the ground, and therefore do not leave much time for defenders to change places and assume more advantageous positions for reception. In other words, they can no longer play the ball standing or facing the net. Therefore, players are forced to react and move quickly and to use specific techniques, for example, falling. **Setting while falling** is an action where the player plays the ball with volley or dig set with one or both hands while at the same time rolling.

The **volley while falling** sideways or backwards is used in situations in which easy, but low balls or higher balls that are further away than normal, must be played. It is suggested here, that in order to achieve greater accuracy players should use a two-handed volley instead of a dig set. This is all the more applicable when one considers that the latest rule changes allow double contact during a volley if the player is in an unfavourable position relative to the ball.

The **two-handed dig set** while falling sideways or backwards should be used when balls are played at hip level or lower. This also applies to the defence of low and fast moving balls. The **one-handed dig set while falling**, is used when the dig set with two hands is no longer possible. This happened when all low, fast travelling balls far from the body which are saved either with one-hand dig to the side of the player or with a dive in front of the player (see LO 13/Session 1).

Simplified, it can be said that as playing techniques the reverse volley or sideways are employed by **setters and covering players**, while the dig set while falling sideways or backwards is used more by the **covering players and backcourt defenders. Attacker coverage** is a team tactic whereby players cover their own attackers close up. Also, further away in two concentric 'semicircles' in order to save, receive and pass the deflections (see Fig. 253). Therefore, these shots are grouped into the basic situation defence/reception and pass, and should be seen in relationship to the formation of blocking and backcourt defence. The technical prerequisites for the reverse volley or sideways set with two hands while falling which are necessary for effective attack coverage are given in Session 1 and in connection with the EXAMPLES for the one-hand dig set while falling sideways. In Session 1, drills precede games, as it is difficult to simulate these falling techniques, and because the risk of injury is too great if they are used too early in competitive situations by players of limited experience.

Movement Progression of the Two-handed Volley and Dig Set while Falling Backwards (see Figs. 254 and 255)

The movements are the same as for the front volley and dig set except for the elements of impetus and positioning at the moment of ball contact (see LO 1 and 4). In order to get underneath the low travelling ball the player takes a low ready position placing one foot in front, while the body weight is shifted back. The player moves his buttocks close to the heel of the back foot and thus initiates the rolling movement The ball contact is executed while falling and directly prior to hitting he back on the backcourt. Because of the lack of leg involvement, it is not possible to have a full body extension, therefore the ball is contacted solely with arms. In the case of volley the missing leg extension is compensated for by the arm bending and extending which adds to the impetus gained.

1. The players stand in a line. Setting is executed in front of the receiver so that the player should set while falling after moving forward to the ball.
2. Variation of 1 above throw/set is directed next to the receiver so that the player can play while falling after moving sideways (see Fig. 262).

Game Form 1.1

Individual and partner competition
Method:
Targeted setting and setting while falling backwards and sideways from a short distance. The ball first thrown by the player himself and later by someone else is played to a certain target (wall, basketball board, goal hoop, etc). The winner is the player or partners with the highest hit quota from ten (twenty) tries. (This can be used as "Learning Check".)

Game Form 1.2

Game structure: 1:1
Court size: 4.5 x 3m
Only one ball contact is allowed. The ball is put into play using a volley.

Variations on Game Form 1.2

1. **Court size:** 2.25 x 4.5 m, later 3 x 6 m
2. **Game structure:** 2:2
Court size: 6 x 3m, later 6 x 4.5m, afterwards 9 x 3m
Follow the rules of the game, whereby the ball can only be put into play either with a serve or also with volley.
3. As above, but on court sized: 3 x 6m, later 3 x 9m.

Coaching Point:
- The volley while falling has priority to dig set in standing.

Observation Points:
- Are techniques while falling or other defence techniques used because the players are in bad alignment or are unwilling to move?
- Has the introduction of dig and volley while falling improved reception/defence or setting?
- Is setting or attack possible after the execution of the falling technique?
- Have the techniques while falling clearly improved the repertoire of techniques and manoeuvres of the players, both at the first and second ball contact?

- Is the two-handed dig set while falling sideways mastered so well that the one-handed dig while falling sideways can be taught afterwards (see "Session Example") based on the familiarity with the movement?

Game Form 1.3

Game structure: 3:3
Court size: 6 x 4.5m, later 6 x 6m
Rules:
Play the rules of the game with special rule that one additional point is awarded for each successful attack which is preceded by reception and pass, or by setting while falling (see Fig. 259).

Errors/Corrections of Setting while Falling Backwards and Sideways

! Errors in Cross Co-ordination which also Include Injury Risks
- The buttocks are not held close enough to the heels when falling.
- The arms do not follow the setting movement but are used to stop falling.
- The player falls from a high, as opposed to a low starting position, or from straddle instead of step position.
- The player makes no changed step, or one which is too short and cannot keep the body's centre of gravity between his legs.
- The player does not hold his head (chin) close to his chest when rolling, but holds it back.

Suggested Solutions:
Simple or preparatory drills:
1. Roll forward or backwards on a mat.
2. Backward roll with return to upright position over one foot (possibly with the help of the partner).
3. Shifting body weight from one leg to the other in wide straddle position (possibly with the help of a partner).
4. Practice the lunge step sideways followed by a body turn, rolling away and backward rolling, later rolling away and roll over.
5. Practice of falling backwards and sideways after movement forwards (possibly with marking for the order and length of steps).
   - As drills 4 and 5 above, but on a mat with a held ball, throwing of the held ball while falling and playing the resting ball.
   - The above exercises, but without a mat.

a) the attack runs via position III,

b) the opponent forms a good and active double block.

c) There are players on the own team with very strong jumping and hitting abilities, who can carry out short spike/smashes straight down.

d) Setting is close to the net.

When forming attacker coverage the following **principles** are to be considered:

* The covering player assumes a low position, the backcourt defender, a medium-low, ready position.

* The players in the second line stand opposite gaps in the first line to watch attacker, ball and block.

* Difficult balls are played high and more to the middle of the court, easy balls are targeted to the setter in the forward zone.

* The formation of attacker coverage is accomplished in stages, i.e. the backcourt defenders move up first to make their running distances shorter, then the setter directly after setting, and afterwards the attacker not being used as the last one.

* If the attack does not run directly near the net, the attacker himself is involved in the coverage in terms of self-coverage. This applies only to off-the-block balls which fall to or in front of the attacker between him and the net.

Explanation

After reception/defence and passing of the ball, the backcourt players move up to the middle of the court in order to cover their own attacker, together with the forward players, who guard against deflections after setting. In doing so, the player(s) adjacent to the attacker, and the backcourt player in position VI up take on direct coverage. The backcourt players V and I and, if necessary, the forward

Fig. 265

players II and IV take on indirect coverage of the attack. In the case of attack with outside position on IV there is 2:3 attacker coverage (see Figs. 265/263), while for attack in the middle there is 3:2 coverage (see Figs. 253/264). The covering players assume a low or medium-high ready position and play the off-the-block balls high to the middle of the court, or to the setter at the net in order to build up a systematic offence.

Game Form 2.1

Game structure: 3:3
Court size: 4.5 x 4.5m
Objective:
The players should experience the function and the use of attacker coverage with position VI up, and be able to employ both formations according to the game situation in order to save deflections and to start a new attack.

Rules:
- In each group there are two forward and one backcourt player (position VI).
- The ball is brought into play with an attack after setting, where the attacker is covered. The defending team of three forms a double block with coverage.
- The winners are the group which can execute the most successful defence actions of off-the-block balls within a given time (5 or 10 minutes).

In order to create such situations, the attacker has to deliberately play or hit to the block (see Fig. 266). After breaks in play the right of attack goes to the other group which rotates one position before attacking.

Coaching Points:
- The players form two concentric circular lines around the attacker.
- Player VI moves up to the attack line after the first pass, and to attacker coverage after setting.
- The setter moves to cover the attacker immediately after setting.

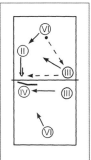

Fig. 266

Coaching Points:
- Backcourt players I and V move up to the middle of the court after the first ball contact, and to backcourt defence after the second ball contact.
- Position yourself as a player in the second defence line (backcourt defence) to the players of the first line (coverage) and stand opposite gaps.
- As a covering player, play difficult balls high to the middle of the court and easy balls high to the setter in the forward zone.

Observation Points:
- Because of problems in the technical execution of attacker coverage is it necessary to refer to Session 1 of LO 11?
- Do the covering players need help in making themselves understood?
- Is the block so effective that the necessity of attacker coverage is clear for the players?
- Are the techniques while falling used mostly in attacker coverage?
- Has the introduction of attacker coverage contributed to game responses marked by intensive movement?

Game Form 2.3

Game structure: 6:6
Court size: 9 x 9m
Rules:
- Play according to rules of the game with the following special rules:
- The ball is put into play not with a serve, but with an attack shot after setting.
- Each line-up is practiced five times, then the teams rotate.
- After thirty attacks the right of attack changes.
- The attack runs from the 5-player pattern, and from block and backcourt defence with the player VI up via setter III (see Fig. 270).
- Later via setter II, with attacker coverage accordingly (see Figs. 263 and 264).
- Each error by a team earns a point for the other team.

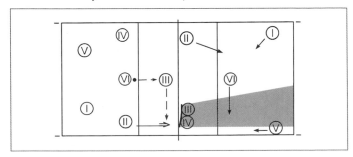

Fig. 270

- Additional points are awarded for each successful blocking, or attack, after attacker coverage.

Observation Point:
- Are the players able to play off-the-block balls so that systematic transition to a repeated offence can progress?

Variations on Game Form 2.3

1. The ball is thrown into court from the outside by the coach, so that a continuous rally can be played (see Figs. 271 a/b).
2. As 1 above but the ball is thrown first either to the right or left court, later at random. After ten throws there is a rotation.
3. The ball is put into play with a serve.
4. After five successive serves, the right to serve changes, i.e. there is a rotation. Points can only be earned by the serving team, additional points by both teams. Sets or rounds are played.
5. Play a game 6:6 according to game rules but with additional points (see Figs. 272 a/b).

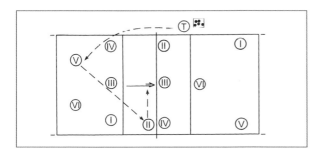

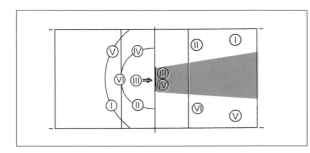

Figs. 271 a/b

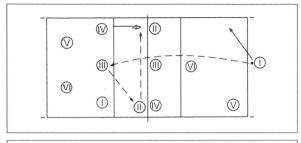

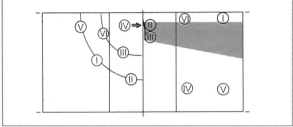

Figs. 272 a/b

Observation Points:
- Has training attacker coverage improved the flow of play?
- Is it necessary to additionally train one-handed setting while falling sideways (see examples), as balls travelling sideways and far away are not reached, and they cannot be received/defended using the falling techniques learnt so far?

Learning Check-List:
1. Students are able to answer test questions (with the help of sketches if necessary) concerning:
   a) The different formations of attacker coverage.
   b) The importance of attacker coverage and the responsibilities of each player, especially with regard to their responses in coverage and backcourt defence.
   c) Attacker coverage according to setting and attack zone.
   d) The transition possibilities from defence to offence.
2. Free game observation of attacker coverage, with player in position VI moved forward, taking into consideration the above-mentioned aspects (b and d).

Errors in the Line-up of Attacker Coverage
- The players stand behind each other instead of in between the gaps.
- The players assume wrong positions and distribute themselves irregularly on the covering lines.

Suggested Solutions:
- Renewed theoretical discussion on attacker coverage formations and the responsibilities and tasks of the players.
- Drills without the ball, where the various attacker coverage formations are taken up at a given signal. Afterwards practice with the ball. In this drill the block deflected balls are first simulated with dump/tip-attacks backwards by the attacker, later forward, with tools (wall, soft floor mats; blocked blocking player on box).
- Drills with attack shots to triple block and adequate attacker coverage, whereby the second ball gets into play simulating an off-the-block ball situation when the block is not successful.
- First, attacker coverage is practiced only with attacker covers. Later, with both attacker covers and backcourt defenders. Offence runs first via positions II and IV (2:3 attacker coverage), later via position III (3:2 attacker coverage).

! **Errors in the Basic Response of Covering Players**
- Non-situation-specific use of the supporting defence techniques, because there is no movement to the attack zone, or a movement is too late.
- Upright instead of medium-high or low ready position.
- Too low or quick setting, instead of receiving the ball as late as possible and passing high.

Suggested Solutions:
Partner/group exercises whereby directly blocked balls are simulated with dump/tip attacks (lobs):

- 'A' plays a long pass to 'B' and runs after it to take over attacker coverage. 'B' dump/tip attacks to 'A'; 'A' plays difficult balls high, easy balls to 'B' and reassumes his starting position. 'B' plays a long pass to 'A', etc. At first only one player (A) covers (see Fig. 273), later both players cover in turns after every long pass.

- A' plays a long pass to 'B'; 'C' moves to the ball to cover the receiving player 'B', 'B' dump/tip attacks to 'C', who returns high; 'B' plays to 'A'; 'C' follows, etc. (see Fig. 274).
- Same as b), but two players cover alternately (see Fig. 275).
- Three players stand in a triangle. 'A' plays a long pass to 'B', 'A' and 'C' cover the attacker, 'B' dump/tip attacks to 'A' or 'C', who return the ball high.

Afterwards the players quickly reassume starting positions, 'B' plays a long pass to 'A' or 'C', etc. (see Figs. 276 a/b).

- Same as d), but with four players in square (see Figs. 277 a/b).
- Drills against the wall.
  After setting comes a drive or jump set (dump/tip attack) to the wall. The covering players pass the deflected balls so that offence can be repeated (see Figs. 278 to 280).

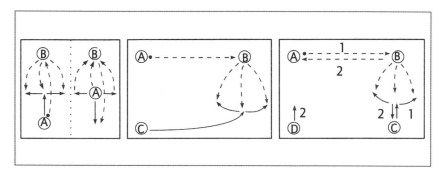

Fig. 273   Fig. 274   Fig. 275

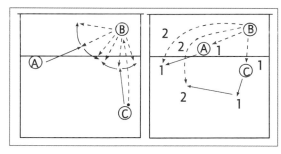

Figs. 276 a/b

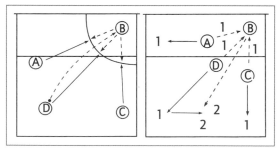

Figs. 277 a/b

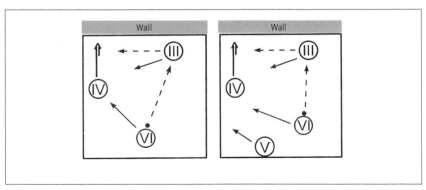

Fig. 278 a   Fig. 278 b

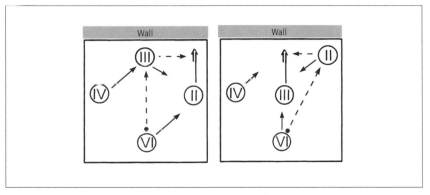

Fig. 279 a   Fig 279 b

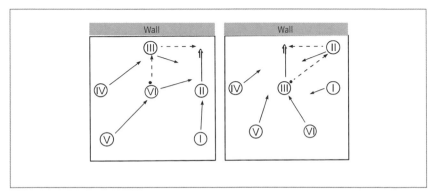

Fig. 280 a   Fig. 280 b

In the case of the attacking team playing a high set over a short distance, using a penetrating setter, high passes are recommended to the outside position IV as inaccuracy increases with playing height. Also, the opposing double block can be easily formed (in position III even a triple block) and thereby negating the advantage of the penetrating game (see Fig. 283).

Explanation

In expectation of the medium-high set, the attacker stands in ready position close to the attack line. Shortly after the set is executed, he runs to take the shot and, depending on the set height and direction, he adjusts his stride, jump and spiking/smashing.

Fig. 283

Game Form 1.1

Game structure: 2:1
Court size: 3 x 9m
Objective:
As an attack variation, players should experience playing an attacking shot after medium-high set and use it according to the game situation. This can speed up the attack and to surprise the opposition.
Rules:
1. One setter and one attacker play against a backcourt defender (see Fig. 284).
2. The attacker spikes/smashes five times (ten times) in succession after a medium-high pass and earns one point for each hit to the opposing court which cannot be saved with two-handed ball contact.

3. After five (ten) hits, the players change their positions.
4. The winner is the player with the most effective shots in one, two or three sets.

Coaching Points

- As an attacker, when there is a medium-high pass from a short or medium distance, the player should run directly after setting.
- As a setter, when there is a medium-high set from a short distance, stand under rather than behind the ball.
- As a setter, when there is a medium-high set from a short distance, use the arms more than the legs.
- As an attacker, when there is a medium-high set, approach earlier than in the case of a high set.
- Choose the take-off place and time according to set width and height.
- Remember that the change in the set height does not require any change in the execution of the attacking shot movement.

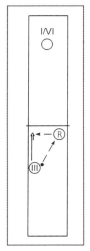

Observation Points

- Is it necessary to refer to EE of LO 4./Session 2 and LO 9/Session 1 because there are major problems in the accuracy of movement and targeting of the medium-high set over short and long distances.
- Additionally, LO 5/Session 2 because there are basic problems in the execution of the frontal attack shot movement?

Fig. 284

Variations on Game Form 1.1

1. The setter gets to the setting place after a short run, he starts directly after the ball has been thrown by the attacker, first a) from the sideline (parallel to the net), later b) from the attack line (facing the net) (Fig. 285).
2. Game structure 3:3; court size: 3 x 9m, later 4.5 x 9m. Game form and variation (1) with one additional player as attacker in position II. The attacker

Session 2: Offence Progression from 5-Player Pattern via Position I

Action Sequence

According to the **rules of the game** no player is tied to his position after the serve, i.e. each player can take any other position and thus assume other responsibilities. This rule is restricted, however, in that a backcourt player is not allowed to hit the ball over the net from the frontcourt onto the opposing court, i.e. he cannot act either as attacker or blocking player, but may only be used as a setter.

The **5-player pattern with offence via backcourt players** is basically the same as that via frontcourt players (see LO 7 and 9). Only the manning of the pattern positions and the offence progression with setter position between II and III are different. The forward line of the pattern is formed by the players in positions IV, III and II and the back line by positions VI and V. Keeping to the line-up rules, during the penetrating game the setter in position I stands hidden behind the player directly in front of him at position II and is thereby not involved in service reception (hence the term **'hidden penetrating game'**). Directly after execution of the serve setter I runs outside past position II to the **setting position between II and III** (see Fig. 291 a). From here the setter (especially right-handed attackers) can set to positions IV and III favourably on their hitting side. It is also an advantage that he can watch positions IV and III and can play facing the net; he can also set to position II using a reverse set from short and medium distances. It is also important that the setter does not hinder the attackers in their manoeuvres (approach) (see Figs. 281 and 291 b). He can watch the responses of the blocking player in position III, and can take this into account for his own setting. The **penetrating action** is aimed at hindering the formation of the opposing double block. This can only be achieved when the whole net width is used in the offence progression and all attackers are used variably and evenly.

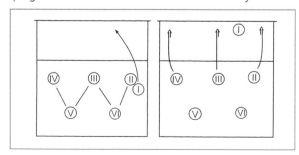

Figs. 291 a/b

An important aspect in the success of the offence with penetrating setter is the response of the attacker in position III. He is the first choice for an attack as he has a favourable position in relation to the setter. Number III has direct eye contact with the setter and can attack from very close to him. He thus succeeds in tying up the blocker in position III of the opposing team, so it is possible that in the case of a deceptive reverse pass, or medium-high set to position IV, that blocker may not be able to join the double block in time. Similarly, an attack via the centre may be done in such a way (dig set) that the formation of the double block to the attacker in position III becomes difficult or can be prevented altogether. Based on the teamwork of setters and attackers the following situation is created:

a) The setter heads for the setting area directly after execution of the serve.

b) The setting place between positions II and III is reached before service reception.

c) The reception and pass are directed to the penetrating setter.

d) The attacker in position III is first to run to the attack, shortly afterwards the player in position II runs up and lastly the attacker in position IV (see Fig. 292).

e) The setter sets and takes over the function of the player in position VI who has moved forward in attack coverage (position VI takes over the responsibility of position I). The attacker is covered and backcourt defence is formed (see Figs. 293 a-c).

f) After a break in play setter I and position VI return to their positions.

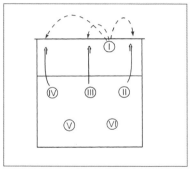

Fig. 292

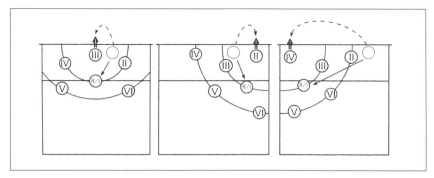

Figs. 293 a-c

Variations on Game Form 2.1

1. The ball is put into play with a serve and the attacker is covered. The setter takes position VI after setting (Figs. 296 a-c).
2. The attack via backcourt player I only takes place once on each side of the court after that a double block is formed and an attack via frontcourt players (III and II) is set up (see Figs. 296 d-f).

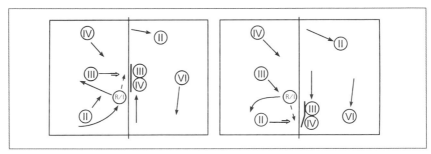

Fig. 296 a   Fig. 296 d   Fig. 296 b   Fig. 296 e

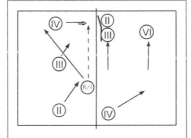

Fig. 296 c   Fig. 296 f

Game Form 2.2

Game structure: 3:3
Court size 4.5 x 6m, later 6 x 6m
Rules:
1. Each group plays with two frontcourt and one backcourt players (position I).
2. The attack runs from two player pattern with setter 1, during play via frontcourt players (see Figs. 283 and 297).

Observation Points:
- Is it necessary to refer to Session 1 as well as to EE of this LO, as there are problems in the teamwork reception/setting/ attack?

- Does the setter make himself known when running, e.g. by calling "runner"?
- Do the attackers let the setter their readiness and the expected set?
- Do the attackers in positions IV, III and II move in the right order?

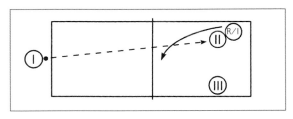

Fig. 297

Variations on Game Form 2.2

1. Game Structure: 4:4; Court size: 4.5 x 9m, later 6 x 9m.
   Two frontcourt and two backcourt players play (see Fig. 298 a).
2. Variation (1): with three front- and one backcourt players (see Fig. 298 b) on playing court 9 x 6m.

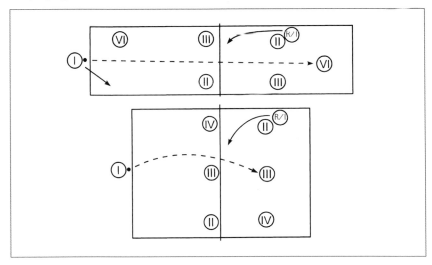

Figs. 298 a/b

Coaching Points

- As a runner, directly after setting, move to the rear of your own attacker to take on smash/spike/smash coverage, and play on as player in position VI up.
- As a runner keep an eye on the ball and your team-mates.

Errors/Corrections of Penetration Game

! Errors and Their Possible Solutions in the Basic Line-up of the 5-Player Pattern and in the Movement and Accuracy of the First Pass

See EE of LO 9/Session 2, taking into account, however, the changed alignment of the players in the pattern formation with setter in position I.

! Errors in the Execution of Running Play

- The starting place of setter I is adjacent to, instead of behind, position II (line-up error).
- The runner starts too early and makes mistakes in the line-up, or too late, instead of directly after execution of the serve (timing error).
- The starting place of setter I is too far behind position II instead of up close.
- The running route goes inside past position II, instead of position II outside.
- The runner expects the first pass at positions II or III instead of between positions II and III.
- The setter does not move away from the net, neither after executing the set to cover the attacker nor in game situations in which he cannot set because of an inaccurate first pass.

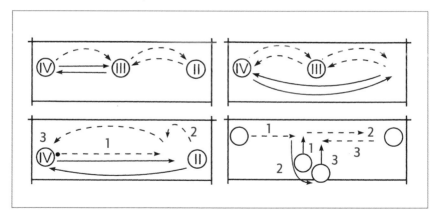

Figs. 300 a-d

Suggested Solutions

- Drills where variable setting is executed after finished movement, if possible make use of the net (see Figs. 300 a-d).
- Play a game with each other, making sure of correct responses of the setter, e.g. game 2:2 on court size: 3 x 4.5m with one front and one backcourt player;

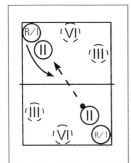

game 3:3 and 4:4. When the third contact is a jump set and no blocking is formed to allow practice of running from the two or three player pattern each time the ball crosses the net (see Fig. 301).

Fig. 301

! Errors in the Teamwork between Setter and Attacker
- The three attackers do not take their ready position to attack.
- The attacker in position III is not the first to offer to attack with a medium-high pass.
- The attacker in position II expects a high instead of medium-high set, and does not act according to the situation.
- Setter I does not vary the set height according to the attack position.
- The setter plays inaccurately, i.e. in between the attack positions, and does not take into consideration the hitting hand side of the attacker and the width of the set.
- The attackers are not ready to act as setters in the event of inaccurate first passes.

Suggested Solutions:
1. Renewed theoretical discussion of the movements of the backcourt runner with the help of various tools taking into account the order of the actions of each player.
2. Drills where the attack builds up from the two and 3-player pattern with setter I. First the ball is put into play by a pass to the runner, later with a serve. To start with, the attacker runs via a predetermined position, later via all positions at random.
3. See also Session 1/LO 12.

! Errors in Attacking Coverage
- The setter and position III and/or II hinder each other in attacker coverage.
- The setter stays at the net after setting, instead of covering in the function of backcourt player VI.
- The players take the wrong positions for attacking coverage.

Suggested Solutions:
- See EE of LO 11/Session 2 with regard to attacking coverage after penetrating (see Figs. 293 a-c).
- Games among themselves (3:3 and 4:4), in which first only attackers in position III or II can be used and covered, later all attackers at random.
- All group and team drills for penetrating with attack against a standing block (blocker, mat, wall, player on box, etc.) to encourage attacker coverage situations.

Learning Objectives 13:

Dig Set Falling Forwards – Double Block and Backcourt Defence with Position VI Back Deep

Fig. 302

Situational Analysis

The attack using a runner, and the use of an attacking shot after a medium set (see LO 12) help improve the second basic situation set/offence. To counter this action the improvement of the defence is required. This can be achieved first by reinforcing backcourt defence while maintaining double block. **Blocking and backcourt defence with position VI moved back** (Fig. 302) satisfies this requirement, as all the players not involved in double blocking, act as backcourt defenders (see LO 8), i.e. when there is a double block there is no block coverage. Block coverage is then handled by backcourt player I or V as **backcourt defence** and by the blockers themselves as **self-coverage.** Beginning in the double block, the block and backcourt defence with position VI back requires greater athletic, technical and tactical skills of the players, than the formation with position VI up.

This is based on the following:
- The defence area of each backcourt defender is larger, especially to the back.
- In defence the backcourt defenders and also the blockers, mainly have dual functions.
- The responses of the backcourt defenders, changes according to the location of the opponent's attack.
- The mastery of defence techniques in falling, above all of the dive, should be considered an important prerequisite.
- The above factors require a higher level of anticipation, speed of reaction and agility.
- The transition from defence to offence via the second pass from the backcourt is made more difficult. There are generally several players who could do the setting and fast communication between the players is necessary.

The factors mentioned above mean that the mastery of defence techniques in falling is an important prerequisite for blocking and backcourt defence with position VI up.

In this context, the requirement to dig or set while falling forward viz. **the dive**, are of great significance as they allows reaching and saving balls at a greater distance (see Fig. 302). Therefore, the learning of the dive is emphasized in Session 1. As was already the case when teaching dig set in falling backwards and sideways in LO 11, the dive must also be taught first with drills, and later used situation-specifically in game forms.

In Session 1 both the one- and two-handed dive are described. The mastery of the two-handed dive should be considered as an important requirement for learning one-handed setting.

In the framework of Sessions 1 and 2 the teamwork of backcourt defenders among themselves, and that of backcourt defenders and blocking players, is dealt with especially thoroughly. In this context the questions of self-coverage and attack progression after defence are stressed.

Session 1: Dig Set in Falling Forward

Fig. 303

Action Sequence (Fig. 303)

The player moves with short, quick running steps to the travelling ball and **jumps** from a low ready position **from a single leg take-off, travels low, forwards and downwards.** In the case of a two-handed dive, the ball is played with the forearms

or hands. If a one-handed dive is executed, the ball is played with the back of the hand, while the free hand helps in absorbing the floor contact

In the two-handed dive, **impetus** is given mostly with arm involvement, while in the one-handed dive it is with both arm and also wrist involvement. At the **moment of ball contact** the player assumes a hollow back position (**arch**) which is done by holding the head back at the neck and

Fig. 304

- Drills without the ball in which the gliding movement, and later the jump and gliding movement, are practiced first from a position on the stomach, then on the knees, then half kneeling, half crouching, and afterwards from a low ready position.
- Drills where balls (e.g. tennis balls) held by the player himself, then stationary balls (e.g. on a ball rope line) and finally easy, accurately thrown balls are played high from a dive, first from a standing position, later after movement. Balloons and slow motion balls are also very suitable for this.
- If necessary, provide floor markings for the order of steps and the take-off or playing location.

! Errors in Take-off

The player jumps:
- from too upright a starting position.
- upwards instead of low and forwards.
- from two legs instead of from one.

Suggested Solutions:

All the drills mentioned already are suitable.

! Errors in Choosing Take-off Area
Suggested Solutions:

- Drills where balls are at first thrown, then played evenly, later varied are played from a dive after movement, first after walking forwards, then after running forwards (if necessary with markings and swinging balls).

! Errors in Impetus

- No wrist bending, when doing the one-handed dive.
- Arms not used in dive.
- Too early or overhasty arm and wrist involvement in order to use the hands as early as possible in landing.

Suggested Solutions:

- Repetition in particular of drills in which stationary or easily thrown balls are defended in dive making sure of a long, low jump with contacting of the ball after the extending phase shortly before landing.

Session 2: Double Block and Backcourt Defence with Position VI Back/Deep

Action Sequence

Blocking and backcourt defence with position VI back is a favourable defence formation against teams with exceptionally good attackers and/or those that mainly spike/smash and do less dump/tip-attacks. In comparison to LO 8 in which backcourt defence with position VI back and, the single block were presented and dealt with, the **double block and backcourt defence with position VI back** result in the following changed responsibilities and responses.

- The players not involved in blocking, are involved in backcourt defence.
- Block coverage is shared by several players:
  - **a)** the blocking players themselves (self-coverage)
  - **b)** the backcourt defenders in position I or V (backcourt defence).
- Almost all the players have double defensive responsibilities owing to the lack of block coverage:
  - **a)** blocker block and own block coverage.
  - **b)** backcourt defender backcourt defence and distant block coverage.

- The lack of close block coverage creates larger defence areas forward. This requires, on the one hand a higher level of athletic ability, and on the other, additional defensive techniques and therefore, there are special requirements regarding individual-tactical responses.
- The separation of the overlapping defence responsibility areas is difficult and requires a high degree of communication in the teamwork of backcourt defenders.

The **starting position** of the players in backcourt defence with position VI back and double block is the same as with single block (see Fig. 313). With **double blocking in position VI Up** (see Figs. 312 and 314) the players undertake the following defence responsibilities:

- The **blockers in positions III and IV** block and cover the area directly behind the block with self-coverage. When dump/tip-attacks are being played over the block, defenders try to turn during landing while watching the ball trajectory. The block-free forward player covers the block and defends the forward zone on his own side. They are in a low 'ready position' in order to be able to defend the ball even before floor contact.

! **Errors in the Teamwork of Blockers and Backcourt Defenders**
- The backcourt defenders in position I and V do not orientate themselves to the block and do not stand outside the block screen.
- The blocking players disturb each other in self-coverage after blocking or in setting after defence.
- The blockers and backcourt defenders disturb each other in covering dump/tip-attacks.

Suggested Solutions:
- Drills where balls are deliberately thrown, played or hit to the overlapping zones of defending players: later each situation is separately repeated several times, later practiced alternately at random.
- Drills where systematic offence is built up after defence with forward or back-court players.
- The above drills with block formation.

! **Lack of Anticipatory Abilities among Backcourt Defenders**
- The backcourt defender does not watch and disregards, or watches too late, the setting place and type, in addition to the attack location and the response of the attacker as well as the response of the blocker.

Suggested Solutions:
- Training of movement observation with the aid of picture series, film and video recordings of different movements in setting and offence, whereby the player has to anticipate the expected intention shortly before the action is executed.
- Drills with offence and defence, when setting and attack form is deliberately varied so that the defensive player learns to take the different forms of response into consideration. In this drill he has to signal acoustically or visually the expected intention of the attacker, and/or make this clear by acting accordingly:
  - The higher the attacker can extend, the shorter the ball can be hit to the backcourt, i.e. the further forward the backcourt defender has to move.
  - The further the set is from the net, the longer the ball trajectory of the attack shot is, i.e. the less the backcourt defender moves forward.
  - The better the block is formed, the more varied attacks can be expected, i.e. the backcourt defender takes a medium-low ready position in order to make movements to all directions possible.
  - The closer the ball is set to the net, the greater the chance of successful blocking; consequently off-the-block balls or tactical hits are to be expected by the attacker. Therefore the ready position should not be too low.

Learning Objective 14:

Frontal Overhead Serve – Attack Coverage 2:3 and 3:2 with Position VI Back

Fig. 329

Situational Analysis

The **frontal overhand service** represents an important **tool of the attacking side**, which if introduced too early can cause problems and disturb the desired balance of the two basic situations, namely the flow in play and enjoyment of playing the game. It also creates problems for the reception of the overhand serve that is made more difficult as the ball flies faster and thus harder. Having said this, it must be said that learning the movement itself is relatively easy. The server has up to eight seconds to execute the action, to determine the target and to implement his plan. All the above, plus the fact that the server can act independently of his team-mates, make for quicker mastery of greater individual tactical ability as a server than, for example, as a receiver, setter etc. The above rationale justifies the late introduction of the different types of overhand serve, especially as long as priority is being given to general training. The above considerations underline even more the requirement stated in LO 2 of consistently **teaching the serve** in conjunction with reception. At this stage it is also essential to combine service reception with the transition to offence including attacking coverage.

In order to keep errors in serving as low as possible, initially the serve should be executed from the middle of the serving area behind position VI. As soon as serve and reception are reasonably well mastered the place should be changed or varied.

The introduction of **attacker coverage 2:3 and 3:2 with position VI back** proves necessary at this stage, as LO 13 focused on blocking and backcourt defence with position VI back and therefore the attacking coverage should be adjusted to this defence formation. Session 1 to a large extent builds on Session 1 of LO 2 and Session 2 on Session 2 of LO 11.

Session 1: Frontal Overhead Service

Action Sequence (Fig. 330)

The player stands with his feet shoulder width apart; right-handers have the left foot placed forward. If possible, the ball is thrown with both hands in the extension of the body axis. The throw is "timed" so that the arm can be moved back and the hitting movement can be smoothly executed and the ball is contacted with the arm extended above the body. When **throwing**, the ball is contacted as late as possible (above shoulder level); the non-hitting arm is held in front of the body to balance and the hitting arm is bent behind the head. At the same time the hitting shoulder is moved back while slightly bending back and turning the upper body. The **impetus** to the shot is given by bringing the shoulder forward (upper body), by arm and leg extension and by wrist involvement.

Fig. 330

Meanwhile the elbow is pulled over shoulder level. The ball is **contacted with the palm** whereby the ball is hit from behind and below. The ball is brought into forward rotation, in particular through **use of the wrist** – therefore the term "serve with effete" (meaning the spinning of the ball) – which stabilizes its flight.

Explanation

The server observes the line-up and responses of the opposing team in order to decide where the overhand serve should be placed. He throws the ball in the extension of the body and hits the ball with extended arm from behind and below to the target with the aim of scoring a direct point or to make the systematic progression of the counter-attack more difficult.

Fig. 331

Game Form 1.1

Game structure: 1:2
Court size: 2.25 x 6m
Objective:
The player should experience and use the overhand forward serve as an adequate offence technique in order to prevent the opponents systematic offence progression, to make it more difficult or to score a point directly, taking into consideration the opponent's responses and his own abilities.
Rules:
1. Groups of three play against each other.
2. Player 'A' executes an overhand serve targeted to player 'B', who receives the ball
3. and passes to frontcourt player 'C'.
4. 'C' sets 'B', who executes a jump set targeted to 'A' so that he can catch the ball (Fig. 332 a).

Session 2: Attacker Coverage 2:3 and 3:2 with Position VI Back

Action Sequence

The players covering the attack, form two concentric semi-circles, one close and the other deeper around the relevant attacker. The responsibilities, the importance of close and distant coverage and the actions of the players are the same as in case of attacker coverage with position VI up (see LO 11).

The significant difference is in the position of the player in position VI: while he is position VI up, he always acts as player in close coverage; when he is position VI back, he always act as **instant coverage**. When there is an attack, the **backcourt player in position I**, moves to positions II and III, while the **backcourt player in position V** moves to position IV for **close cover** of the attacker (see Figs. 329 and 338 a-c). It should be noted that the form of attacking coverage with position VI back is irrespective of the type of offence action, i.e. whether they run via the front or the backcourt player (penetrating setter).

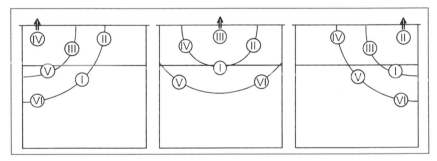

Figs. 338 a-c

Explanation

During transposition to attack from defence with position VI back, the backcourt players in positions I and V position themselves forwards to the middle of the court in order to take on close coverage of the attack. The backcourt player is normally in position I when the attack is from positions II and III, and the backcourt player in position V in case of attack from position IV. The backcourt player in position VI always takes over the area behind the backcourt player who is involved in close coverage of the attacker and covers the second defence line. In an attack from positions II and IV the team forms attacking coverage of 2:3, in attacks from position III that of 3:2 in order to save deflected balls (see Fig. 339).

Game Form 2.1

Game structure: 3:3
Court size: 3 x 9m
Objective:
The players should experience the responsibilities and the use of attacker coverage with position VI back, and must be able to use the formation according to the game situation to save block deflected balls and to introduce a new attack.

Fig. 339

Rules:
1. Play according to rules of the game with the following special rules:
2. The ball is put into play with an attacking shot after first setting.
3. Dump/tip-attacks and drives are not allowed.
4. One additional point is awarded for each successful offence from attacker coverage (see Fig. 340).
5. Positions III, II and I and that of III, IV and V are filled.

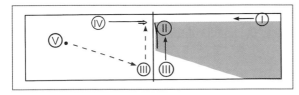

Fig. 340

Coaching Points:
- The backcourt player in position I or V looks after close coverage, while backcourt player VI looks after distant coverage.
- When covering close, take a low ready position about 2-3m away from the attacker.
- Play difficult balls high and from the net, to the middle of the court.
- As a backcourt player in position I and V, move forward early to attacker coverage when your team is in possession of the ball.
- As a backcourt player in position I and V, move early outwards and deep to take on backcourt defence if the opponent has the ball.

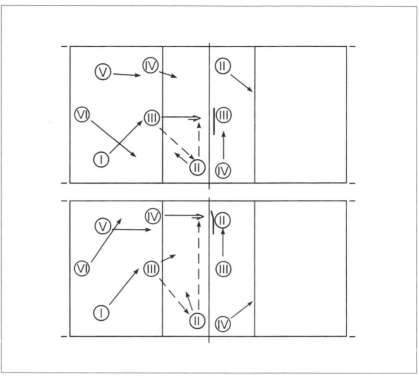

Figs. 343 a/b

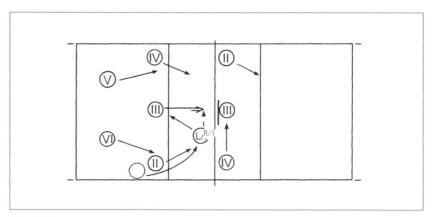

Fig. 344 a

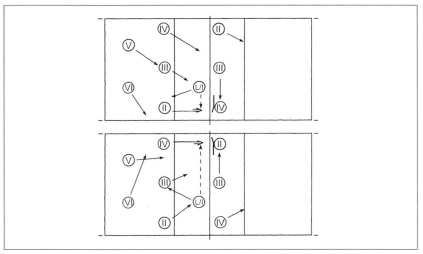

Figs. 344 b/c

Coaching Points:
- As player in position IV moves to position III when attacking, positions I and III move to close coverage, and as they do so the players in position IV and VI move to distant coverage.
- As setter I moves away from the net, immediately after setting to the coverage position.

Game Form 2.3

Game structure: 6:6
Rules:
Play the same rules as variations (1) and (2) of Game Form 1.4 of Session 1 in LO 14 with the following special rules:
1. The ball is put into play not with a serve, but with a spike/smash after setting.
2. One additional point is given for a) successful blocking, b) successful offence and attack coverage.
3. The offence is built up first with setter in position III, later in position II, and finally with penetrating setter I, between position II and III.

Variations on Game Form 2.3

1. The ball is put into play with an overhead forward serve.
2. Game 6:6 played according to the rules of the game.

Coaching Points:
- If the attack runs from position IV as the players in positions III and V move to close coverage, players in positions VI, I and II move into distant coverage.
- If the attack runs from position II, move as player in position III and I to close coverage, and as player in position VI, V and IV into distant cover.
- As distant covering player takes up a position opposite gaps and at a distance of 2-3m from the attack covering players in a medium-low ready position.

Observation Points:
- Is it necessary to refer back to the front underhand serve as there are problems in receiving and passing front overhand serves, and no systematic offence can be built up. Therefore resulting in no possibility to form attacker coverage?
- If there are problems forming attacker coverage, it may be necessary to repeat the techniques in falling sideways and backwards of Session 1 in Learning Objective 11.
- Check that the players have understood the changed alignment in attacker coverage with position VI back. Do they move accordingly?

Learning Check and Errors/Corrections

See also Session 2 in LO 11 with regard to the changed alignment of the backcourt players, primarily in position VI.

Learning Objective 15:
The 0:0:6 System of Play

Fig. 345

Situational Analysis

The **0:0:6 system** is played by teams having six non-specialist players in the team. The first number refers to the number of setters, the second to the number of attackers, and the third to the number of utility players. Therefore, the relationship between the types of players within a team only gives an indication of the actual system of play. Taking into account the athletic, psychological and technical abilities of the players, the system of play provides the foundation for the individual, group and team tactics. It represents a range of decisions on the part of the coach or teacher, the effectiveness of which is greater, the more precisely the system is adapted to the abilities of one's own team and of the opponent, and to all other factors influencing the game. Thus the system of play determines and includes positioning, responsibilities, function and action areas of the individual players, of groups of players and of the whole team in both basic situations of the game. The **0:0:6 system of play** is the simplest, but also the most demanding system. If the players have approximately the same prerequisites and abilities, it can be used at every stage of learning and it is the ideal system of play.

- Is it advisable to use block and backcourt defence with position VI back as the formation of the double block is difficult or is not closed because of the varied attack actions of the opponent and shots can be easily directed into the block screen?
- Is it necessary to give up the formation of the double block for defence with position VI up and change to single block with backcourt defence with position VI back as the opponent attacks with variety and quickly?
- Is it necessary to use block and defence with position VI back as the opponent often attacks with roll shot instead of spike/smash?
- Is it advisable to give up block formation altogether, as the offence progression of the opponent does not allow attack shots?
- Does the offence via position III prove so effective that the formation of a triple block is necessary (see Figs. 345 and 346)?
- Is it necessary to play block and backcourt defence with position VI up as the opponent often fakes or the double block can be easily formed owing to the opponent's volley?
- When there are changes in defence, are the players able to correctly fill their changed position and responsibilities in attack coverage?
- Has the training of universal players contributed to the players understanding game situations more quickly, adapting faster, and successfully taking advantage of the situations?
- Has the equal positioning and equal treatment of all players led to better or worse performance?
- Has the process towards utility players that has created relations among the players themselves, and between players and coach/teacher that are full of conflicts or conflict-free?

Learning-Check
1. Test questions including sketches concerning:
    a) The various types of pattern formations, offence progression from serve reception including attack coverage.
    b) The various types of blocking and backcourt defence, offence progression from backcourt defence including attack coverage.
2. Free play and player observation of the above aspects.

Errors/Corrections of 0:0:6 System of Play

! **Technical-tactical Problems in the Basic Situations and in the Transition from Defence to Offence and from Offence to Defence**

Suggested Solutions:
- Exercises and game forms in which the complete team performs:
  a) only reception with attack progression, attack and attack coverage, or
  b) only attack defence with attack progression, attack and attack coverage and repeats the same alignment several times. Rotation after five or ten executions or as the teacher determines.

About a)
First, only reception and passing of easy and accurately targeted serves, later hard and more difficult serves, afterwards passing and attack, then including blocking and defence, so that attack coverage and transition from attack to defence can be practiced (see example of attack progression with penetrating setter I (Figs. 352 a-c)).

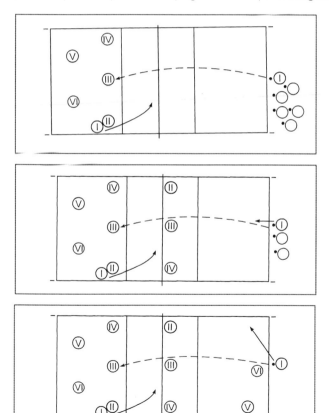

Fig. 352 a/b/c

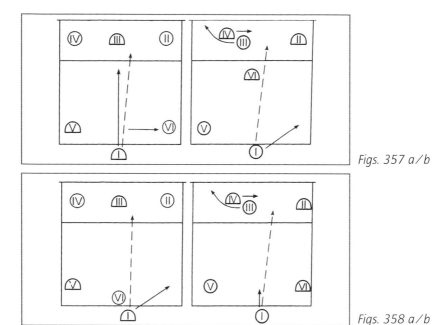

Figs. 357 a/b

Figs. 358 a/b

When the opponent is serving, the setters in the forward zone also change immediately after the serve is executed. The backcourt setters, however, do not change earlier than serve reception and not later than the end of the action, i.e. after the ball has passed over the net (Figs. 359 a/b and 360 a/b).

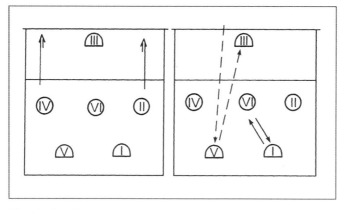

Figs. 359a/b

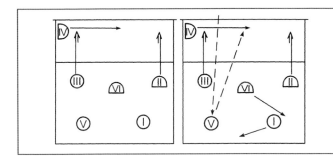

Figs. 360 a/b

When the offence progression is via the backcourt player in position I (see Fig. 356). The runner changes to position VI, after setting, or after attack coverage at the latest. Whereas in play with position VI back he returns to his position I, after attack cover.

Situational Analysis of the 2:0:4 System

The introduction to the 3:0:3 system is primarily the beginning of specialization. On the one hand in order to work out new formations making use of a rough differentiation between the players and their functions. On the other hand, it has the objective of allowing the players to learn to make use of a new role. This is gradual and easily understandable, and thus experience a smooth transition from universal play without position changes to partially specialized play with changing position.

The 2:0:4 system represents a further step towards specialization. Two players act as setters and four players as non-specialist players/attackers. Similar to the 3:0:3 system the 2:0:4 system is first taught with only short position changes making sure to observe attack progression from reception and defence. Taking into consideration the special abilities of the players, the position changes strengthen defence. This leads to a variation in changeover behaviour in the reception and defence situation. Long changes are sometimes necessary with two or three players over two positions. Long changes can also be carried out in two short changes one after the other (so-called "change in stages"). For example, the setter from position IV changes to position III after the opponent's serve, and moves further to position II after setting and covering when the ball crosses the net. The position change when one's own side is serving has the purpose of strengthening first defence and secondly the attack progression from defence. The position on change when the opponent serves strengthens first the attack progression from reception and secondly defence.

A general rule is that changes to strengthen the attack progression and attack always create certain disadvantages for the defence. The change to strengthen the defence has certain disadvantages for the attack progression. Therefore in the case of one's own team serving, or the opponent being in ball possession, the position change should primarily be aimed at increasing the effectiveness of defence. In the case of the opponent having the serve or one's own team having ball possession, the position change should be carried out to increase the effectiveness of the attack.

Action Sequence of the 2:0:4 System

In the 2:0:4 system there are two setters and four general players/attackers. In the basic line-up the setters are positioned diagonally opposite each other so it can be ensured that one setter is always at the net (see Fig. 361 a). Similar to the 3:0:3 system the 2:0:4 system is first introduced with short position changes. The attack is developed from reception in 5-player pattern with setter in position III, and defence is position VI up (setter axis III/VI). The first variation of the 2:0:4 system builds on the following advantages:

1. The setter position is centrally located which allows a relatively long first pass to the setter from all positions.
2. The setter only has to pass over medium distances (2-4m).
3. The setter can easily compensate inaccurate first passes.
4. The second setter in position VI can pass or play any inaccurate first passes thanks to his central position in the middle of the court.

The disadvantages of this variation only arise in the blocking situation if the setter is weak in blocking, compared to his adjacent team-mates, but still plays in the most important blocking position III. At this training stage this potential weakness is, however, consciously accepted because of the above advantages.

On the basis of the setting positions, taking the position changes in III and VI into account, the following formations for reception and defence arise:
If the setters are in positions II/VI (see Figs. 361 a/b), there are no changes whether the own side or the opponent serves.
If the setters are positioned at II and V (see Figs. 362 a/b), there are the following line-ups and position changes:
If the setters are positioned at IV and I (Figs. 363 a/b), there are the following line-ups and position changes:

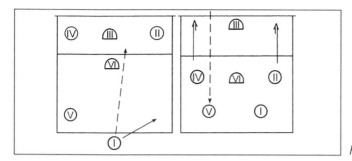

Figs. 361 a/b

Figures 362 and 363 clearly show that in particular when their own side is serving the running distance of the changing players is kept as short as possible and remains the same. All changes when the own side is serving are performed immediately after the serve is executed. Changes during the opponent's serve, however, take place at different times: the forward player changes immediately after the serve is executed (also called "**switching side runner**"). The backcourt setter can change during or after reception, but after attack coverage at the latest the diagonal alignment of the setters means that after the next three rotations identical line-ups are created or repeated.

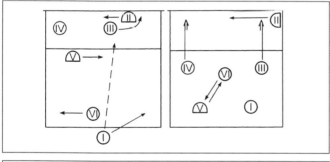

Figs. 362 a/b

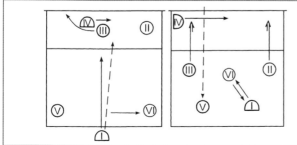

Figs. 363 a/b

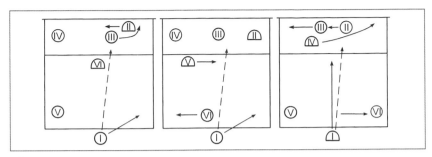

Figs. 367 a-c

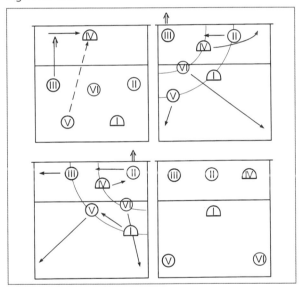

Figs. 368 a-d

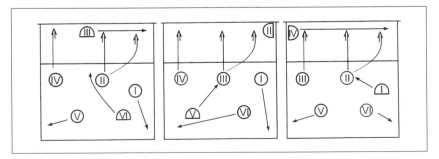

Figs. 369 a-c

Explanation of 1:

With regard to the movements of the players at the net it has to be considered that there is a clear harmonization of the running routes close to and further away from the net. The player changing to position III should always change close to the net and have the shorter running distance. When there is a long change the player changing over two positions should be far from the net

Explanation of 2:

The position changes during one's own serve are performed as shown in Figs. 367 a-c. The position also changes during the opponent's serve that is shown in Figs. 362 b and 363 b. In this variation the change in position II takes place after attacker cover, here shown as an example for switching position IV (see Figs. 368 a-d). This variation becomes more difficult because when the opponent serves, it progresses first via setter position III from reception, and in all other situations from defence in position II. The position change of the forward player in position IV runs similarly to the change in position II and is recommended in certain situations (e.g. left-handed attackers).

Explanation of 3:

The offence progression via setter in position II, both from reception and defence, requires a higher level of technical and tactical skills of the player. With regard to technique the receivers must be able to accurately play the first pass, and the setter the second pass, over long distances (7-10m). As far as tactics are concerned, there are several team-tactical formations in reception which demand a high level of understanding of the game in the teamwork of players (see Figs. 367 a-c and 369 a-c). It is only advisable to use **running play** within the 2:0:4 system if firstly the prerequisites (listed above under point 3) are fulfilled. Plus the fact that if one or both setters can be fully used as attackers. In this way all the advantages of the progression via backcourt players can be fully utilized by using all forward players in offence, shown in the example with runner I (see Fig. 370 a). Here, too, the position changes to the setter axis II/V/(II/I) take place after attacker coverage (Figs. 370 b/ 371 a-c).

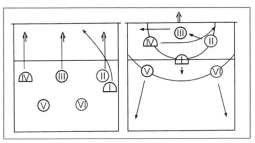

Figs. 370 a/b

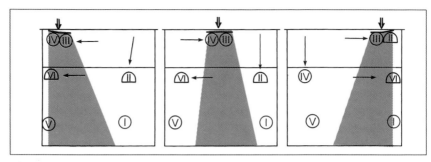

Figs. 371 a-c

A system of play must be developed on the basis of both the technical and tactical conditions of the players and the team and not vice versa. This means it is wrong to press the players into a given system of play. It is the special ability of the coach/trainer to recognize the strengths and weaknesses of his players, and to consider these in the system in such a way that strengths are fully utilized while weaknesses are, at best avoided or if possible remain hidden. Thus it can prove advisable to play with one setter (good blocker) both in reception and defence in position III and with the other setter (poor blocker) in the attack build-up in position II. For this reason the above variations can be tested in order to work out the best system, possibly resulting in a mixture. The following illustrations with the example of a **Reception from the 5-Player Pattern** and the **Defence with Position VI Back** enable a comparison of the various possibilities for action and for decision making.

1. Position changes during one's own serve (Figs. 372 a-c)

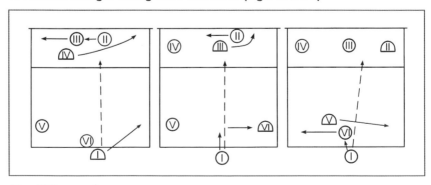

Figs. 372 a-c

2. Blocking and Backcourt Defence (Figs. 373 a-c)

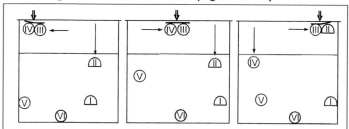

Figs. 373

3. Reception Formation, Offence Progression (Figs. 374-376)

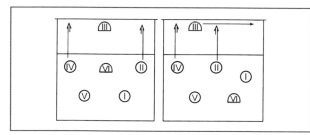

Figs. 374 a/b

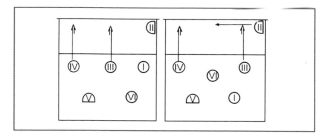

Figs. 375 a/b

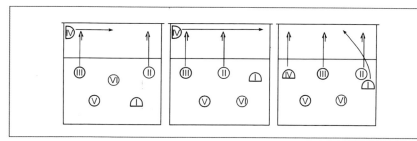

Figs. 376 a-c

4. Attacker cover, position change to blocking and backcourt defence using the example of the movements of Figs. 376 a-c.

In Figs. 377 a-c it should be noted that the position descriptions of the players given in Figs. 376 a-c are still maintained after the change.

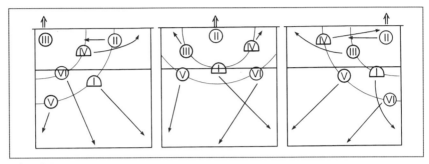

Figs. 377 a-c

A further variation of the 2:0:4 system is the offence progression from the 6-player pattern, in the sense of a situation-specific offence progression. Depending on the serve direction, the offence runs either VI up or backcourt players (see Figs. 378-380).

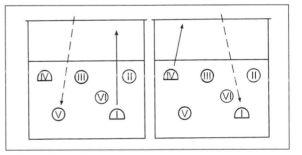

Figs. 378 a/b

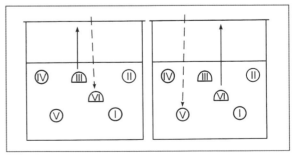

Figs. 379 a/b

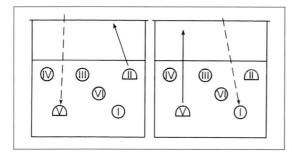

Figs. 380 a/b

Coaching Methodology for the Introduction and Further Development of the System of Play

When developing the system of play, the position changes cause the most problems for players. Therefore it is advisable to first introduce position changes during the team's own serves, as these are relatively easy to learn and perform different visual aids such as sketches, panels, strips, markings etc. make the movements of the position changes and their principles clearer. After this the change of the whole team can be practiced, first without serving, on a verbal or visual signal, later with a serve and opposing players (two to 6-players). In this type of work, players should first think of playing "with each other", later in the sense of playing "against each other".

Stages of Learning to introduce position changes during the opponent's serve within the 2:0:4 system of play:

1. Explanation of and reasons for, the position changes plus instructions on the running routes and the timing of the changes.
2. Test movement of the position changes, initially without the ball, afterwards with balls thrown and caught.
3. Position change during opponent's serve. First serve to a predetermined position/player and offence via predetermined positions. Afterwards varied serves and attacking moves as games one with six.
4. Same as 3), but as game three with six, i.e. two forward players and server. The forward players form a double block so that the receiving team can also carry out the offence progression with attacker cover after first carrying out a change.
5. Same as 4), but as game four with six, i.e. with three forward players and server. The planned position changes during one's own serve in the forward zone can also be practiced.
6. Game 6:6 with inclusion of all position changes, i.e. both during own and opponent's serve.

7. Same as 6), but as game with/against each other, i.e. the first two net passings as before as jump set/drive in the sense of playing with each other, and the following actions in the sense of competing against each other, i.e. with attack shot, fake, etc. Playing with each other allows longer rallies, so that the whole changing responses both during own and opponent's serve with the different offence progression from defence can be trained and checked.
8. Game forms 4-7 as competing against each other.
Especially in the case of a game against each other it is advisable to play with several balls per serve/reception situation to force longer rallies, i.e. when there is a break in play the coach immediately throws a ball into play in order to teach the players all the changes in the different basic situations.

Coaching Points:
- The above game forms are carried out as a so-called "half-court game", i.e. one team first has only serving and defence functions, or only reception/offence functions and then transition to defence. The other group/team has more of an assisting function. Rotation of the group/team takes place either after a given time (2, 5 or 10 mins), or after a given series (10, 15, 20 repeats), or after progress in learning
- In order to create understanding of the new roles by the team-mates and their difficulties in the new positions it is advisable to have all the players act in all situations and roles. This role change can also be practiced on small courts.

9. Drill Training and Competitions 6:6
These serve first of all to test and check the effectiveness of the system of play introduced with special regard to position changes. With regard to the further improvement of a system of play reference is made to the lesson of the 0:0:6 system of play (see LO 15).

All the comments on game forms, observation aids, notes and also EE can be applied.

EXAMPLE OF A LESSON:
ONE-HANDED DIG SET IN FALLING SIDEWAYS

1. An Introduction

The background and underlying theory for this lesson are dealt with in LO 11 and in the chapter "The Book and the Game", especially in the explanations of the learning objectives and teaching models. It is essential that players have mastery of the two-handed volley and dig pass in falling backwards (bw) and sideways (sw) with the two possible techniques of returning to upright position, backward roll or rolling over.

2. Subject and Aim of the Lesson

The subject of the lesson is learning the one-handed dig set by falling sideways and returning to the upright position afterwards (Japanese roll). Here the one-handed dig set should be experienced as a suitable action for defence of balls travelling low from the side and far from the student/player. Fundamentally the students/players should learn to use the one-handed set only in cases when defence/reception with the two-handed dig is no longer possible.

3. Planning and Execution

Tools and Aids
- Series of drawings (see boards).
- At least one ball per two players.
- Net cross or two nets (rope) placed lengthwise in the middle of the hall.
- Goal hoops or basketball hoops.

Sequence of the Lesson
- Preparation, especially of the boards.
- Presentation of the execution and use of the one-handed dig based on the experience with the two-handed dig in falling sideways (use of teaching media).
- Special warm-up (in particular stretching upper and lower limbs; repeat falling movement backwards, sideways and roll over).
- Repeat two-handed volley and dig pass in falling sideways.
- Game series on the one-handed dig in falling sideways.
- Talk about the lesson (eventually learning check).

The lesson can be divided into four *planning* levels:

a) **Game forms:** the game form is a method of emphasizing a particular aspect of the work on which you wish to lay emphasis. The game form is also of special significance as it has a monitoring function for the success or otherwise of the students efforts.

   If there are major problems in the execution of the game form, or if there are basic problems in the movements and actions, reference should be made to the EE in the previous chapter in order to create the necessary learning prerequisites for current activity.

b) **The Objective:** the objective names or describes the desired outcome of the session.

c) **Coaching Points** provide specific guidelines on how to coach and implement the different movement and action concepts. Each coaching point refers to one important aspect, which is significant for the playing of the game.

d) **Observation Points:** the observation aids help both our own observation and observation by others. In this way assistance is given in recognizing the causes of errors in movement and action sequences. Also in checking whether or not the timing and execution of the game form or learning objective are appropriate and correct. Furthermore, by referring to EE specific aid is provided to create the prerequisites for aspects of learning that are missing, or to make good weaknesses or deficiencies. Because of this monitoring function they have a close connection with the notes and represent the link between the game form and practice, problems and how to correct them.

4. Lesson Structure – Game Form

1. Partner Competition

Objective

Players should be able to demonstrate competence in:

- Learning the sequence of movements of the one-handed dig.
- Learning the similarity of the movements of the one- and two-handed dig in falling sideways as well as the two-handed volley pass in falling sideways.

- Identification of timing the ball release in relation to the fall and rolling movement.
- Use of the one-handed dig with adjustment of timing and location in relation to the moving ball.

Court size: 3 x 4.5m
Rules:
Player 'A' stands at the net or under a rope and performs the sideways falling movement of the one-handed dig with one stride to the attack line (five times right/five times left). In doing this the ball is thrown over the net/rope to the opposite forward zone so that player 'B' can catch the ball (one point).

Variations

1. As above, but the ball thrown low by partner 'B' is played in falling sideways.
2. Variation (1), but the ball thrown by the player himself is played sideways.

Coaching Points:
- Make a wide stride with the leg close to the ball.
- Draw the buttocks close to the heels before starting the roll and turn the body in the direction of the game.
- Throw/play the ball up high before the buttocks touch the ground.
- If possible, contact the ball with the palm of the hand from below and behind and use the wrist.
- Roll over the left shoulder in case of a right stride and vice versa.

Observation Points:
- If there are basic errors in falling sideways, it may be necessary to refer to Session 1 of LO 11 (digging in falling).
- Remember that the one-handed dig is to be used for balls that are further away and low.
- Are there problems in executing the one-handed dig because the partner throws incorrectly, as he throws e.g. too close to the body or too high.
- Is the learning transfer from the two- to the one-handed dig in falling sideways recognizable?

2. Game 1:1

Objective
- Players should be able to demonstrate the:
- Use of one-handed dig set from a moving situation.

- Learning of one-handed dig set in falling sideways as adequate technique to play balls that are out of reach, high and away, from the direction of the fall.
- Situation-specific use of the one-handed dig set in consideration of other reception and defence techniques in falling.
- Experience and improvement of rolling (Japanese rolling) to regain quickly ready position.

Court size: 4.5 x 4.5m
Rules:
Player 'A' attacks ten times with a jump set later with a two-handed jump throw. Player 'B' defends. One point is given for each successful offence or for each successful defence (ball is played high).

Variations

1. Game Form 2, but player 'B' earns a point if the saved ball remains on his own court.
2. Variation (1), but player 'B' earns a point if the ball saved and is caught by him after one deflection, remaining on his own court.

Coaching Points:
- Keep an eye on the attackers before ball contact, to identify the ball direction early.
- Use the adequate defence/reception techniques upon contacting the ball according to ball direction and own position.
- Receive high and close balls with volley set, low and close balls with two-handed dig.
- Only use the one-handed dig if two-handed play is no longer possible.
- Remember that the last step to the ball must be taken with the leg closest to the ball.

Observation Points:
- Is it necessary to change the net height or court size so that the offence allows or forces use of the one-handed dig more often and according to the situation?
- Can it be seen that two-handed defence is given priority over one-handed and play while standing is given priority over play in falling?
- Is it necessary to practice rolling separately because the return to the upright position is too slow, or the players are afraid of injury from rolling?

- Is it necessary to replace the game series with a drill series for location (hall/gym) or organizational reasons?

3. Game 1:2

Objective
- Use of the one-handed dig depending on game situation and on team-mates.
- Trying out and learning of targeted defence/reception with one-handed dig to introduce systematic offence progression.
- Improvement of the teamwork of defenders.
- Realize the necessity of quickly regaining the ready position after falling.
- Use of the one-handed dig on small court games during competition.

Court Size: 6 x 4.5m.
Rules:
Player 'A' attacks ten times with jump set or dump/tip-attack, player 'B' and 'C' defend. One point is given for each successful offence or for each successful defence (play the ball high, team-mates catch).

Variations

1. Game Form 3: player 'B' and 'C' only get a point if the saved ball can be returned; first with at least two ball contacts, later with three ball contacts.
2. Game 2:2
   Game Form 3 and variation (1): offence after set by the team-mate.
3. Game 2:2
   Game rules with special rules
   a) Ball is put into play with an attack instead of a serve.
   b) One additional point is given for each successful defence in falling.

Coaching Points:
- Choose the starting position so that the larger defence area is on the better side.
- Choose a starting position so that one has to defend more in front than behind, and more from outside to inside than inside to outside.
- Play high and to the middle of the court, instead of low and in the direction of the net or opposing court.
- Keep an eye on the position and action of the defending players in falling to sense the direction and speed of the ball.
- Even after defending in falling, is prepared to execute the third ball contact, if possibly as an attack shot.

- The player must make himself understood by calling out to team-mates, especially in case of balls in overlapping areas of responsibility.

Observation Points:
- Is it necessary to raise the net/rope because the attacker is too successful and there is no possibility of defending?
- Is it necessary to teach the defence possibilities of the defenders separately?
- Are the players aware that one-handed play in falling is less accurate than two-handed play?
- Have the players realized that by using the one-handed dig they can enlarge their defence area?
- Does the player have to defend in falling
  a) because he has taken a poor ready position?
  b) he has poor positioning on court?
  c) he has deficiencies in speed of movement or reaction and anticipatory ability?

Literature

BRETTSCHNEIDER, W.D./WESTPHAL, G./WESTPHAL, U.: Das Volleyballspiel. Unterricht im Sportspiel zwischen Zielsetzung, Methodenkonzeption und Erfolgskontrolle. Ahrensburg 1976.

CHRISTMANN, E./FAGO, K./DVV (Hrsg.): Volleyball-Handbuch. Reinbek 1989.

DIETRICH, K./LANDAU, G. (Hrsg.): Beiträge zur Didaktik der Sportspiele, Teil 1-3. Schorndorf 1976-1977.

DÜRRWÄCHTER, G.: Volleyball spielnah trainieren. Schorndorf 1974.

FRÖHNER, B.: Spiele für das Volleyballtraining. Berlin 1985.

GÖTSCH, W./PAPAGEORGIOU, A./TIEGEL, G.: Mini-Volleyball. Berlin 1980.

HERGENHAHN, K.-H./NEISEL, G.: Volleyball Spielen Üben Trainieren. Aachen 1989.

IVOILOV, A.V.: Volleyball. Übers. a.d. Russ. v. GUIDO SIJS. Tielt 1978.

MARTIN, D.: Training im Kindesund Jugendalter. Schorndorf 1988.

MEDLER, M.: Hinführung zum Volleyballspiel im 5./6. Schuljahr. Neumünster 1977.

NAUL, R./VOIGT, H.-F.: Volleyballspiel. Sport Sekundarstufe II. Düsseldorf 1979

STIEHELER, G./KONZAG, J./DÖBLER, H.: Sportspiele. Berlin 1988.

VOIGT, H.-F./RICHTER, E.: betreuen, fördern, fordern: Volleyballtraining im Kindes und Jugendalter. Münster 1991.

WESTPHAL, G./GASSE, M./RICHTERING, G.: Entscheiden und Handeln im Sportspiel. Münster 1987.

MEDIA

DANNEMANN, F./SONNENBICHLER, R.: Kinder lernen Volleyball. Heidelberg 1988. Video, VHS E-60, Begleitheft.

GÖTSCH, W./PAPAGEORGIOU, A./SPITZLEY, W.: Technik und Taktik des Sportspiels Volleyball. Teil I und II. Institut für Film und Bild (Hrsg. u. Auslieferung), Grünwald 1987. Videokassetten, VHS in Farbe.

Photo & Illustration Credits:

Cover Photos: Willi Zeimer, Cologne
Drawings: Klaus Bruder
Photos: Willi Zeimer, Cologne (p. 8, 15, 140, 355), Martin Kuck (p. 30, 59, 152, 168, 226, 278), Thomas Maibom, Norderstedt (p.179)
Cover Design: Birgit Engelen, Stolberg

Fit for Success

Alexander Jordan
Train your Back

This book will appeal to all those who want to take care of their backs – either at home, in a sports club, at school or in the gym. Sports leaders, teachers and coaches in particular will find new and varied teaching ideas. A focused programme offers varied and attractive exercises. The emphasis is placed on gentle strengthening gymnastics, supplemented by stretching and mobility programmes.

176 pages
Two-colour print
145 photos, 3 illustrations
Paperback, 14.8 x 21 cm
ISBN 1-84126-073-8
£ 12.95 UK / $ 17.95 US/
$ 25.95 CDN / € 16.90

Fitness

Arz 2 06/02

MEYER & MEYER Verlag | Von-Coels-Straße 390 | D-52080 Aachen, Germany | Fax +49 (0)2 41-9 58 10-10

Fit for Success

Fitness

Georg Neumann
Nutrition in Sport

The book makes recommendations for physiologically useful dietary planning before, during and after training in various sports. It also examines risk-prone groups in sports nutrition. The emphasis is on presenting the latest research on the effects of carbohydrates and proteins and other active substances, such as vitamins and minerals, on performance training. Particular attention is paid to the intake of food and fluids under special conditions such as training in heat, in the cold and at high altitudes.

208 pages, Two-colour print
Some full-colour photos
Paperback, 14.8 x 21 cm
ISBN 1-84126-003-7
£ 12.95 UK / $ 17.95 US/
$ 25.95 CDN / € 18.90

MEYER & MEYER Verlag | Von-Coels-Straße 390 | D-52080 Aachen, Germany | Fax +49 (0)2 41-9 58 10-10

Fit for Success

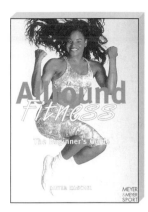

Dieter Koschel
Allround Fitness
The Beginner's Guide

„Allround Fitness" by Dieter Koschel explains his popular and proven approach to fitness, incorporating both basic training principles and the all important element of fun. Designed as a guide for fitness instructors, teachers and personal training, the book describes a well thought out, basic programme consisting of gymnastic exercises, cardio vascular training and relaxation techniques.

120 pages
37 photos
17 figures and 10 tables
Paperback, 14.8 x 21 cm
ISBN 1-84126-011-8
£ 9.95 UK / $ 14.95 US/
$ 20.95 CDN / € 14.90

MEYER & MEYER Verlag | Von-Coels-Straße 390 | D-52080 Aachen, Germany | Fax +49 (0)2 41-9 58 10-10